MARX'S PARIS WRITINGS:
AN ANALYSIS

Marx's Paris Writings:
an Analysis

JOHN MAGUIRE

With an Introduction by
David McLellan

BARNES & NOBLE
BOOKS
10 East 53d St., New York 10022
(a division of Harper & Row Publishers, Inc.)

Published in the U.S.A. 1973 by:
Harper & Row Publishers, Inc.
Barnes & Noble Import Division

© John Maguire 1972

Jacket designed by Graham Shepherd

ISBN 06-494505-7

First published in Ireland in 1972
Gill and Macmillan Ltd
2 Belvedere Place
Dublin 1
and in London through association with the
Macmillan
International Group of Publishing Companies

Printed and bound in the Republic of Ireland
by the Book Printing Division of
Smurfit Print and Packaging Limited

For my parents

Contents

Acknowledgements

IN these few words I can register, but could not hope fully to express, my gratitude to my friends and colleagues in the Department of Ethics and Politics, University College, Dublin. Reverend Professor Conor Martin has sustained and encouraged me both personally and academically to an extent which only those privileged to study under his direction can appreciate. Father Fergal O'Connor O.P. can never, whether he likes or dislikes the product of his efforts, evade the responsibility of having, during the five years when I studied under him, taught me most of what I know. Philip Pettit and Denys Turner, by their persistent and generous over-estimate of my abilities, have widened my horizons: they have been truly guides, philosophers and friends, and I cannot myself measure what I owe them. Professor Patrick Masterson of the Metaphysics Department unfailingly helped me as critic and friend: I can excuse my abuse of his constant generosity only by saying that without it, the whole enterprise would have been significantly less rewarding, if not impossible.

Professor T. B. Bottomore of the University of Sussex responded courteously and helpfully to my many inquiries. Doctor David McLellan of the University of Kent at Canterbury has added a large measure of his personal assistance and encouragement to the indispensable enlightenment which, as will clearly emerge, I have drawn from his published work. He has also honoured me by writing the Introduction to this volume. Mr Andrew P. Johnston of the Milltown Institute of Theology and Philosophy has given me an insight into the experience of philosophy, and broadened my horizons to an extent which emerges in some small measure in this book. Professor Klaus Hartmann of the University of Bonn kindly read and suggested revisions of parts of the manuscript. I am deeply grateful to the staff of the Library, University College,

Dublin, and especially to Miss Mary Hogan, the Deputy Librarian, and Miss Elizabeth Gleeson, now of the Library, Trinity College, Dublin. My uncle, Joseph MacMenamin, has unfailingly helped me with his encouragement and interest, as also with more material facilities. Professor and Mrs Ludwig Bieler have helped and encouraged me in every aspect of my work, but especially in the preparation of translations and the textual appendix. I am, as ever, grateful to the Abbot and Community of Glenstal Abbey, Co. Limerick, and to Dom Paul Macdonnell O.S.B., the Guest Master, for offering me hospitality, peace and friendship at times both pleasant and crucial during the last few years. I would like also to thank the students of Politics in University College for listening and responding to many of the ideas here expressed, and for the critical response which I am confident that their present expression will surely receive. Custom demands that I claim all defects as my own.

John M. Maguire
Department of Ethics and Politics
University College, Dublin

Introduction

THIS is the first full-length study of Marx's Paris writings to appear in English; as such it is exceptionally welcome. The writings of the Paris period—and particularly the *Paris Manuscripts*—are exceptionally difficult. Many passages have the elliptical style and unordered presentation characteristic of notes not destined for publication. They also represent Marx's thought at a time when, under the influence of new political and economic ideas, it is evolving extremely rapidly. There is the further difficulty that the concepts with which Marx is here operating are still very close to his young Hegelian origins and thereby often obscure to the average Anglo-Saxon mind. Thus John Maguire's book, which sets the Paris writings in context and clearly explicates Marx's concepts, is a long overdue aid to the understanding of the young Marx.

But there is a second reason for welcoming a serious study of Marx's Paris writings and that is the intrinsic value of these writings themselves whose publication has caused what could be called a revolution in the interpretation of Marx. From their first publication in 1927 the Paris writings made a swift impression, and interest in the young Marx has since been intense in Germany, France and Eastern Europe. Formerly Marx had been seen as primarily an economist who claimed to have discerned the inexorable laws leading to the collapse of capitalist society. The early writings, however, revealed Marx—at least at that time—as a philosopher, a humanist, even an existentialist. Inevitably the writings were eagerly seized upon by those who wished to use them in political arguments, whether as a critique of orthodox Communist states or as a basis on which to start 'dialogues', particularly of a Christian-Marxist kind.

It is true that some of the first commentators on the Paris writings exaggerated their importance by claiming that they represented the 'authentic' Marx to the detriment of virtually all of his later work; and these same commentators tended to distort Marx's Paris thought by picking out certain themes congenial to themselves and neglecting others. It is, for example, one of the merits of John Maguire's book that he gives full place to Marx's comments on *economic* writers as well as dealing with the more philosophical passages. But although the importance of the early writings has been overstressed, it is equally mistaken to claim that they employ a conceptual system that Marx later abandoned completely. Marx obviously modified radically many of his ideas in the Paris Manuscripts; and their form shows that Marx was far from having achieved the later synthesis of his economic and philosophical ideas. But the study of Marx's later writings and particularly the publication of the *Grundrisse* shows that there is an underlying continuity in Marx's thought: his later specialist economic interests did not obscure the earlier humanist vision. The Paris writings will have an abiding interest for all interested in the study of Marx.

David McLellan
Canterbury, Kent
December 1971

Preface

THIS book is about the following works of Marx: two essays published together under the title 'On the Jewish Question'; an essay entitled 'Contribution to the Critique of Hegel's Philosophy of Right: (Introduction)'; and, by far the largest of the works, a set of manuscripts called variously the Paris Manuscripts, the 1844 Manuscripts and the Economic and Philosophical Manuscripts (*EPM*). The first two essays were drafted in Kreuznach in 1843. They were published, together with the third essay, in the *Deutsch-Französische Jahrbücher* (Paris 1844). The manuscripts were written in 1844, but not published during Marx's lifetime. I shall use the term 'Marx's Paris period' to refer to the time during which the essays were published and the manuscripts written.[1]

My chief reason for writing about these works is their own intrinsic interest and importance. Had they been the only works written by Marx, the world would have been impoverished but would nevertheless have these writings as some consolation in its loss. Like all works of merit, they are of perennial interest as reflecting the attempt of an original and profound thinker to come to grips with his world and its problems. But for us, removed less than a century and a half from the context of Marx's critique and ideals, they hold an even more immediate interest. This is so largely because of what Marx tried to do—to grasp the human significance, the determining forces and the real possibilities of the new world emerging through the economic and political revolutions of his period. Without adulating him as a latter-day seer, we must still admit that in our time his critique as presented in these works stands, as he himself said of the German philosophy of his time: 'at the centre of the problems of which the present age says: *that is the question.*'

There is thus a real continuity, or rather a unity, between

the problems with which Marx grappled, and those which face us today. The greatest contribution which the writings of the Paris period make to the discussion of these problems is their showing us Marx's first attempt at a task which governed his concerns throughout his life: to evolve an empirically-based understanding of man which would ask the right questions of his world, and point to the real possibilities of humanising that world. In these writings industrial society is given significance and criticised in terms of a frame of reference based on an anthropological understanding of human needs and potentialities. As we share many of the same problems which faced Marx, we can benefit from the precise content of his writings and its application to our own societies; but even when that content has lost its topical reference, the method of analysis from which it arises will survive as an irreversible gain.

It would however be improper, and in the contemporary situation of scholarship and controversy impossible, to consider these Paris writings simply and solely in their own right, without reference to their relation to the rest of Marx's works. This is so for two reasons, which we might characterise as strong and weak reasons. The *weak* reason is one which would hold of any writer who produced a large output covering, as did Marx, a wide area of inquiry: to treat one work in isolation is to misconceive both the range and the development of his thought: '(we must set) each work in the whole movement, the basic movement of his thought, which emerges as thought *in* movement and thought *of* movement, which develops by posing problems, unmasking contradictions, working out solutions which are themselves contradictory and which lead on to new questions, that is to say *dialectically*.'[2]

In the case of Marx, however, there is an additional, a *strong* reason, for not treating any of his works in isolation. This is because there is deep controversy as to what, if anything, constitutes the unity, the 'guiding thread' of Marx's total output; the two sides in the debate may best be described as Continuationists and Dichotomists.

The Dichotomist thesis should come first, as it raises the problem. In its most generalised form it holds that Marx's *oeuvre* displays a point, or even points, of discontinuity, in a sense other than the obvious one that all writers develop, change their emphasis, and modify their style of presentation. We may fix such points of significant discontinuity formally by saying that they are such as to make any unified reading of that total *oeuvre*, any reading which regards as continuous works which are divided by such a point, either empty and superficial or downright misleading: the break is such as to make it impossible for Marx himself, the Dichotomist or the reader to regard the world simultaneously through the eyes of 'early' and 'late' works; still less possible to assent simultaneously to the visions of the world thus attained.

Dichotomists, as their name would suggest, fall into two camps. We may consider firstly the Late Dichotomists. These assert that there is at least one decisive break in the alleged continuity of the *oeuvre*, and regard the works subsequent to that break as being in fact more true to the spirit of Marx's mature outlook. Along with this judgement of fact there goes frequently a judgement of value, in the sense that the later works are regarded as being by some standard *more authentic*. The Soviet and Eastern European commentators who rule Marx's early writings out of court do so on the grounds that they are infected with 'idealist terminology', 'Hegelian overtones' or some similar sign of intellectual infantilism. One may suspect that this judgement of value is not unrelated to the fact that the appearance of many of the early writings as late as the 1930s has called into question dogmatic interpretations of the significance of Marx's thought, which interpretations were regarded as the touchstone of intellectual, and more importantly political, orthodoxy in those countries. Another Late Dichotomist, the French author Louis Althusser, has put forward a much more profoundly argued case to the effect that it was only after the 1840–48 period that Marx shook off the Hegelian cast of mind and adopted a rigorously scientific, post-humanist outlook; this break, he claims, is so decisive that even the recurrence of the same *words* in 'late' as in 'early' works hides a profound equivocation as to the meaning of the concepts which they signify.[3]

The Early Dichotomists, as might be expected, agree with the Late in alleging a decisive break in the sequence of Marx's works. They differ, of course, in that they stress the early works as more worthy of attention. Interestingly enough, they are often quite ready to agree with the Late Dichotomists on the question of *fact*: in the light of their judgement of *value*, to the effect that the 'early' is the 'essential, authentic, humanist' Marx, they are often quite prepared to concede that he may have done any number of indescribable things once he had lost his authenticity. A good example of such a treatment, based almost entirely on the Paris Manuscripts, is Erich Fromm's *Marx's Concept of Man*, his long introductory essay to the volume, with this title, containing the United States edition of Professor Bottomore's English translation of the Paris manuscripts.[4]

It is, indeed, on these very manuscripts that the Early Dichotomist case has most heavily rested. This is understandable in the light of the fact that they were not published in any language until the Russian edition of 1932 under the direction of Riazanov. In the next fifteen to twenty years, they exploded on the intellectual horizons both of Soviet dogmatism and of disillusioned anti-Stalinist Marxists in the Western countries. This long delay in publication, whatever its motives, compounded the fact that, even if all had been known, Eastern 'heretics' and Western humanist socialists alike tended to emphasise the admittedly considerable differences of both content and terminology between the manuscripts and, say, *Capital*; in some cases, indeed, Late Dichotomist arguments are put forward simply as a rejection of the triumphant discovery of the 'early Marx'.

But enough of mere narrative: is there conclusive evidence for either side? Firstly we may note that it is not surprising that two sides did in fact emerge. Perhaps chiefly responsible for this is the uneven emergence of Marx's works: the last came first, and the first last. Thus for a long time the only works known with any degree of depth of study were ones which appeared after 1848. These were undoubtedly of a 'scientific' nature, and quite unlike the more 'philosophical' style of the sketchily known and superficially judged earlier works. Even without ideological and political complications such as arose during the Stalin era, conditions of scholarship alone would have yielded the legitimate impression of a vast difference in content and presuppositions between *Capital* and what was known of the pre-1848 writings. Given the coincidence of the conditions of ideology and those of scholarship, it is still less surprising that this difference was even more emphasised when quite a number of the earlier works did at last begin to emerge. Late Dichotomists found conclusive evidence of the tainted nature of these works; Early Dichotomists found a basis for their rejection of the version of Marx administered by their political and intellectual opponents.

We may thus discern, behind the later accretion of interest and prejudice, a real problem of reconciling the works of two periods in Marx's life: there is truth on both sides in the controversy. The most decisive development in the last ten years or so has been, not a change in or addition to the evidence on either side in this controversy, but rather a recognition that the controversy itself was in important respects unreal. As early as 1956, Jean-Yves Calvez in his *La Pensée de Karl Marx* presented a reading of a large number of Marx's works, stretching from the early 1840s to *Capital*, arguing incidentally that there were many significant elements of continuity. His interpretation has been contested on a number of grounds but the work raised the question, and showed the possibility, of a complete, integrated reading of all of Marx's *oeuvre*. More recently, Avineri's *The Social and Political Thought of Karl Marx* (C.U.P. 1968) has dealt explicitly with this question of continuity, and shown that many of the alleged oppositions between early and late works are incorrect or exaggerated. One reason which Avineri advances is that 'much of what is traditionally considered orthodox Marxism is based on the more popular of Engels's later writings. If they seem to differ widely from those of the Young Marx, the conclusion usually drawn from this disparity is a statement about a difference between the early and the later Marx.'[5]

But even more decisive in the development of the Continuationist position has been the integration into Marx-studies of a work which played little role, even in Continuationist presentations, until recently: *Fundamental Traits of a Critique of Political Economy*, usually referred to by the first word of its German title as the *Grundrisse*. This work, the fruits of Marx's reading and reflection during the fifteen years preceding 1858, did not appear in the West until 1953. Martin Nicolaus first stressed its importance in English in an article in 1968, when there was still no adequate English translation. He argues that: 'between the early Marx and the mature Marx the *Grundrisse* is the missing link.'[6] He illustrates continuities between the Paris Manuscripts and the *Grundrisse*, as well as pointing out differences and intervening developments. He also shows the continuity between the *Grundrisse* and *Capital*, thus arguing for a fundamental continuity that permits important elements of difference and development within the total corpus. McLellan, in the Introduction to his translation of selections from the *Grundrisse*, argues that: 'Marx's thought is best viewed as a continuing meditation on central themes broached in 1844, the high point of which meditation occurred in 1857–8. . . . Marx constantly used, and at the same time revised, material from an earlier date: he used his notebooks of 1843–5 while writing *Capital*.'[7]

The point about these developments is that they undermine the very terms of the old debate about the young and the old Marx: they show up as radically deficient the reading on which both sides based their cases. Thus to call the opponents of the Dichotomists 'Continuationists' is in a way to do them less than justice: if the question had never been raised, they would not have had to give an answer, negative or positive, to it. Their position *vis-à-vis* the Dichotomists defines only part of their total contribution, which is the positive one of working towards a comprehensive reading of a vast system of related but differing and developing writings. This is not the place to re-present the evidence on which McLellan establishes this continuity, showing that Marx himself never rejected his early writings in the fundamental sense in which he was thought to have done so. It is enough for the purpose of this Preface to note that the assumptions of the traditional 'Old/ Young' debate have now been radically challenged, and that the evidence points to a much greater continuity and unity between the different stages of Marx's thought than that debate assumed.

This brief review of the present state of Marx-studies is intended to set the present analysis of the Paris writings in perspective. Even the most convinced and recalcitrant

Dichotomist must regard the *EPM* as an important stage in Marx's development. He commits himself logically to at least the minimal thesis that all of Marx's works are the works of the same man: even if he regards the later works as embodying an uncompromising rejection of the presuppositions of the earlier, it is still crucially important to know precisely *what* was rejected; what we reject defines our rejection, in the sense that there is no such thing as pure, abstract 'rejection'. It is vitally necessary to know whether what Marx rejected in his past, if he did reject it at all, was 'Hegelian idealism' rather than, say, medieval Christian theology or oriental mysticism.

But to the extent that contemporary evidence points to continuity in Marx's work, the Paris writings acquire a positive importance, rather than the merely negative position which the Dichotomist would accord them. In so far as there is a link of common questions and a fundamentally unchanged method of approach running throughout Marx's whole output, the Paris writings are of importance as revealing Marx's first tour of the course: he begins to evolve a position of his own, to make clear his positive and negative relations with the thinkers who influence him. But if continuity rather than rupture is the case, then we may well ask: 'why spend much time on what is in fact only a preliminary sketch of a later, fuller treatment? If the works are basically continuous, what makes these writings of more than specialist, scholarly importance?'

The answer lies in that intrinsic feature of Marx's work which lent plausibility to the impression of a radical break between his early and mature writings: the fact that what Marx actually produced reflects a narrowing of scope, from the rejection of a whole philosophy and elaboration of an alternative with which the Paris manuscripts are concerned, to the detailed economic analysis of a given type of economic system contained in *Capital*. As we shall see in Chapter 3, Marx's Introduction to the Paris manuscripts envisages a vast work embracing a critique of economics, politics, law, religion and so forth, the whole to be capped by a critique of Hegel's philosophical system. The manuscripts do not fulfil this intention, nor, as McLellan convincingly demonstrates, does the *Grundrisse* exhaust all of Marx's ambitious outline project.

Still less does *Capital*, the precise relation of which to the projected whole is discussed by McLellan in the texts already referred to. If then there is unity between the 'different Marxes', and if at the same time the later writings such as *Capital* represent the fulfilment of only a section of the intended total treatment, it becomes vital to see such later writings in the context of the projected but unfinished totality in which they were meant to appear. This is so for two reasons. Firstly, there will by definition be themes in the original outline and draft which are not treated at any great length in the later output; to ignore the earlier work is thus totally to overlook these themes. Secondly, such an incomplete perspective is necessarily a distorted one on even the works which it does cover, as it inevitably suggests that some topics have been discarded or even rejected in favour of what actually did get treated in the later output; for example, there is the impression that Marx was a 'philosopher' in his early writings, and 'became' an 'economist' in the later. It should be seen from my analysis that the first half of this impression is inaccurate; the evidence to which I have already referred would refute the second half. As McLellan argues: 'the *Grundrisse*, then, are as Hegelian as the " Paris Manuscripts ", and their publication makes it impossible to maintain that only Marx's early writings are of philosophical interest, and that in the later Marx specialist economic interests have obscured the earlier humanist vision. The early writings contain all the subsequent themes of Marx's thought and show them in the making.'[8]

I have already said that my chief reason for writing this book is the intrinsic merits of the works with which it deals. But I consider the controversies which I have just outlined to be of importance because the whole of Marx's work is of importance, and it is important to know whether he radically changed his mind at some stage, and if so on what points. The purpose of this book is to present as clearly and as usefully as possible the contents of Marx's Paris writings. The controversy about the interpretation of all Marx's writings is introduced here in order to show the context in which an understanding of the writings analysed acquires significance, even urgency, as an intellectual objective. Without ignoring the controversies, I do not intend in this work to further one or more of the many

sides involved: in essence I am concerned to answer the
question: what does Marx say in the Paris writings?

But there are two possible objections to this endeavour. The
first, that it has been done before, is I believe not true. In
Chapter 1 I briefly review the treatment of the topics under
discussion in the available literature, and I do not know of any
work which even in intention goes into the Paris writings at
such length and in such depth as it is my intention to do here.
The second objection is that I should let the works speak for
themselves, and spend my energies exhorting others to read
Marx himself rather than interposing my own presumptuous
mediation. My answer is that the writings which I am
analysing are far from speaking for themselves. The essays
on the Jewish Question and on Hegel's *Philosophy of Right* were
indeed prepared for publication, and published by Marx
himself; nevertheless even in the form of a final draft they are
epigrammatic and compressed, in a style characteristic particularly of Marx's early period. Even where there is no
substantial problem of interpretation or evaluation, their
meaning does not leap to the mind. The position is even more
difficult when we come to the manuscripts. These were not
written in final draft form, but rather composed as Marx
grappled with the problems which they discuss. Much of their
contents is 'thinking out loud' transferred to paper. Many
underlying themes emerge only in their application to specific
topics: Marx is not a man to give us a preliminary outline,
far less a set of definitions, of his fundamental concepts and
presuppositions. While an elucidation of the manuscripts'
contents does not require reading into them things which are
not there, it certainly requires an ordering and interpreting of
those contents. I shall not give examples of this point as the
whole book is, I would suggest, an illustration of its validity.

While the first and chief aim of the book is to elucidate the
Paris writings, we cannot and should not avoid some further
questions. Firstly, there is that of the background, of Marx's
development prior to the Paris period. While Chapter 1 is
not intended as a replacement of other works and parts of
works, referred to in that chapter, which deal with the same
matters, it is intended to give a fairly complete outline of
Marx's intellectual development prior to 1843, and of the

context, social, political and intellectual of that development. Similarly, Chapter 6 discusses some basic themes and questions of interpretation raised in the analysis of the Paris writings, with references to other works of the 1844–48 period, notably the *German Ideology* (1846) and *Poverty of Philosophy* (1847). The reasons for doing so are stated at some length in Chapter 6; here it will suffice to say that I discuss these works because some topics raised in the Paris writings are elaborated in them, and also because some problems of interpretation are brought fully to light only when the Paris writings are compared with other pre-1848 writings. Thus one of the purposes of the book is to set the works which it analyses in the context of the other early works of Marx. To which period in his life do I apply the terms 'Young Marx' and 'early works', and what are my reasons for doing so?

There are three possible answers:

(*a*) The terms could be taken as referring to Marx's Young Hegelian period, in which case the *Essays and EPM* would be seen as the first writings of the 'Old' Marx. I do not adopt this definition, because Marx's works in the period 1841 to 1843 are neither systematic nor positive. Many, such as the newspaper articles, are on specific topical issues. Others, such as the *Critique of Hegel's Philosophy of the State*, are negative rather than positive in intention. It is only in the Paris period that Marx comes near to a consistent and positive statement of his own ideas.

(*b*) The terms could be taken as referring to the period preceding the collaboration with Engels, in which case the *Essays and EPM* would be the last writings of the 'Young' Marx. I do not adopt this definition either. My reason is that, although Marx has begun to make positive statements of his own views, he is still, in the period 1845 to 1847, engaged in the process of disentangling himself from the legacy of his Young Hegelian past. Thus these years represent the coincidence of negative and positive developments in Marx's works. It is only after this period that both Marx and Engels turn aside from the negative task of refuting Bauer, Stirner, Feuerbach, Proudhon and others, and devote their time and energies to a positive development and statement of their own views.

(*c*) I thus regard the term 'the Young Marx' as referring to the whole pre-1848 period. This is the definition implied by the range of works discussed in, for example, Delfgaauw's *The Young Marx*. Equally, therefore I regard the term 'Marx's early works' as referring to the works which I have described in outline on pages 7 and 8.

Once more I stress that it is not the purpose of this book to substitute for, or duplicate, the work of other authors who have dealt with the young Marx. Nevertheless, I believe that the work would be incomplete if it did not give an idea of the main themes and points of interest in Marx's works of the pre-1848 period; without referring to these works it would give an incomplete and at certain points misleading impression of the significance of the Paris writings.

Lastly, if, as I have said, these writings are of interest primarily because they say important things about important problems, it is necessary to summarise and criticise the attitude which Marx takes to these problems in them. The final chapter will raise the questions of the contents, merits and defects of Marx's philosophy of man as it emerges in the Paris writings.

I have throughout employed the translation given in T. B. Bottomore (ed. and tr.), *Karl Marx: Early Writings* (London 1963). That book is devoted to a complete and continuous translation of the works with which we are concerned: the Essays and the Paris Manuscripts. There are also translations of these works by Milligan, Easton and Guddat, and McLellan, but none of these three versions is complete and continuous.[9] I have read Bottomore's translation in conjunction with the German originals as given in *Karl Marx, Friedrich Engels, Historisch-Kritische Gesamtausgabe: Werke/Schriften/Briefe*. This edition, which I shall refer to as *MEGA*, was started in 1927 under the editorship of D. Riazanov of the Marx-Engels Institute in Moscow. Of the forty volumes projected, only the first twelve were published. A fuller discussion of the availability and merits of translations is given in Appendix 1.

MEGA is divided into Sections (*Abteilungen*), Volumes (*Bände*) and, on occasion, half-volumes (*Halbbände*). A section and volume will be referred to as, for example, *MEGA* 1, 1. Where a half-volume also is specified, the reference will be,

for example, *MEGA* 1, 1, i, or *MEGA* 1, 1, first half-volume.
Bottomore's translation will be referred to as Bottomore.
Quotations from this volume will be given in the text, followed
directly by a page-reference preceded by the letter B: for
example, (B 197). In some cases I have referred to major
works of Marx, Hegel, Bauer and Feuerbach without giving
exhaustive references. In such cases, the reader who desires
fuller information should consult Appendix 2 below. Where a
book is referred to, and has already been referred to in the
same chapter, it may be given as, for example, Avineri, *op. cit.*
or the title may be abbreviated. Titles of articles from books
or periodicals are given in quotation marks in the first reference
but subsequent references in the same chapter may be given
by abbreviating and italicising the title of the article, preceded
by the author's name.

I

Marx's Young Hegelian Period and Outline of the Early Writings

> Marx's work lends support to Aristotle's saying
> that to understand a thing one must study its
> origins.
> D. MCLELLAN,
> *Marx before Marxism*

KARL Heinrich Marx was born in 1818 at Trier in Germany. He escaped many of the disadvantages at that time connected with Jewish parentage because his father, Heinrich Marx, had renounced the Jewish faith and become a Protestant. Karl grew up in an atmosphere dominated by Kantianism and free-thinking, which flourished in the clubs of which his father was an active member. From 1830 to 1835 he studied at a grammar school in Trier, and in 1835 enrolled at the University of Bonn.[10] Here began the long conflict between his wide-ranging intellectual interests, and his father's desire that he should study and practise the legal profession. In 1836 he moved to Berlin, of which university city one of Marx's future associates had written that 'in no other university does such general industry rule, such striving for knowledge, such peace and quiet as here.'[11]

Berlin was the intellectual centre of the time. It was here that Hegel had held the Chair of Philosophy, and had produced not only the last of his published works, but also those parts of his philosophy which were subsequently reconstructed from his pupil's lecture notes.

The Young Hegelians

Since Hegel's death in 1831, there had been a void in German philosophy, of which the philosophers themselves were aware. At first there was unanimity 'that Hegel's philosophy was the ultimate one and that all that was left for his pupils to do was to work out its implications in the various fields as yet only touched upon by Hegel himself.'[12]

However, as soon as this 'working out' began, the unanimity quickly gave way to bitter conflict. The first controversy arose over the question of religion. D. F. Strauss' *Das Leben Jesu*, published in 1835, was the opening shot. Strauss, who had studied under Hegel, attacked the very foundations of theology, and interpreted the gospel narratives as projections of the collective imagination of the people, as myths. He was opposed by a group who earned the name of 'Right' Hegelians. This group insisted on maintaining theism, and also supported the notion of the Christian state, in which religion was established and supported by the political power. Many younger Hegelians supported Strauss' 'Left' interpretation, and these formed the school which came to be called the Young Hegelians.

This was the circle with whom Marx associated in his Berlin days. McLellan describes them as a group of young men, almost all, including Marx himself, from fairly well-to-do families, whose chief common bond was their belief in the power of philosophical criticism as the effective enemy of the evils of the time. Kamenka tells us that at this period of his life, Marx shared this faith that 'it was sufficient to expose the contradictions of empirical reality and to hold up against them the truly rational.'[13]

Just as the unanimity of the whole post-Hegelian school foundered on the question of theism, the unanimity of the Young Hegelians themselves did not last for long when confronted by the political realities of the time.

While Frederick William III ruled Prussia, political problems lay more or less dormant. Hegel's philosophy was fashionable, and it was tacitly accepted that this philosophy did not conflict essentially with the constitution of the Prussian state. Just before this monarch's death in 1840, however, the unorthodoxy of the Young Hegelians had begun to lead them into controversy both with the political authorities and with the orthodox interpretation of Hegel on the religion question. The accession of Frederick William IV at first appeared to promise an improvement from their point of view, especially as there was a relaxation of press censorship. In 1841 a leading Young Hegelian took advantage of this relaxation to found a newspaper, the *Rheinische Zeitung*. Ruge had edited the earlier *Hallische Jahrbücher*, which journal had reflected the uncertainties and contradictions of the whole Hegelian school by including contributors of all shades of opinion from Strauss' bitterest opponents to his stoutest allies. The *Rheinische Zeitung* embraced only those who had opposed orthodox Hegelianism, although, as imminent events were to show, this was almost their only unifying characteristic. The relaxation under the new monarch did not last for long. He was committed to the idea of a divine right of kings, and anxious to build a political system which would establish Christianity firmly as the state religion, which would be instilled into his subjects. The leading theoreticians behind this grand design were Ludwig von Gerlach and Friedrich Julius Stahl, who 'automatically distrusted any doctrine which . . . subordinated the Church to the State.'[14]

From this time on, the Young Hegelians could not avoid confrontation with authority, because the existence of the state was regarded by authority as synonymous with the maintenance of traditional Christianity. This being so, the Young Hegelians could no longer claim to be 'purely religious' thinkers who had no political interests: their religious radicalism, in a state which identified religion and politics, necessarily involved them in political controversy. In 1842 Bruno Bauer, who had spearheaded the atheistic element in Young Hegelian thinking, lost his *licentia docendi*. Ruge, refusing to accept Prussian censorship of his journal, moved to Dresden and renamed it the *Deutsche Jahrbücher*.

In 1841 Ludwig Feuerbach had published his *Das Wesen des Christentums* in which he made a radical attack on philosophy as such, calling for a materialism which would direct attention to the real, perceptible world, and away from the realms of idealist speculation. Feuerbach's influence on the Young Hegelians was great, but soon proved divisive. Bruno Bauer led a rival group, called *Die Freien*, (The Free Ones) at Berlin. This group disdained the Feuerbachian onslaught on philosophical speculation. They grew increasingly disenchanted with political activity, believing that nothing worthwhile could ever be hoped for from the 'masses'. In 1843 they published the *Allgemeine Literatur-Zeitung*, which the *Rheinische Zeitung* frequently and bitterly accused of irresponsibility, political unrealism, and even nihilist subjectivism.

Although the opponents of Bauer were united in being influenced by Feuerbach and in their rejection of the Berlin group, this was about as far as their unanimity went. When clashes with authority drove most of them into exile, a group went to Paris and started the *Deutsch-Französische Jahrbücher*. A split developed between those who applied Feuerbachian ideas only to religion, and those who went further and developed a critique of the very foundations of the democratic theory of the state. The Paris group did not long outlive the fast-disintegrating Berlin group, and by 1845 the Young Hegelian movement, in so far as it merits such a title, was dead. As McLellan says: 'above all a movement of intellectuals, with no large-scale backing among the people, and no interests in common to hold them together, they were doomed to disappear along with their organs of publicity.'[15]

MARX'S YOUNG HEGELIAN PERIOD

We have already seen that in 1841 Marx shared the one basic creed of the Young Hegelians, that rational criticism was the only effective weapon against an irrational world. When the split developed over Feuerbach's ideas, Marx joined the pro-Feuerbach faction, and became involved in editing the *Rheinische Zeitung*. At this stage he had already developed his interest in political as distinct from religious controversy. He published a number of articles in the newspaper, in which this interest clearly emerges.[16] In one article he discusses a debate in the Rhenish Diet on freedom of the press and on publication of Diet proceedings.[17] He supports a free press, basing his argument on democratic principles. He asks whether political authority believes that it is divinely inspired. He argues that freedom follows logically from the nature of the press, whereas censorship is opposed to it. The central category in the article is, indeed, the idea of liberty itself:

the absence of liberty is thus for man the real danger of death.[18]

In another article he replies to the *Augsburger Zeitung*, a newspaper devoted to the conservation of the established political system, which had charged the *Rheinische Zeitung* with communism.[19] Marx defends his newspaper on the grounds that what it said was a purely neutral statement of fact, that communism was a matter of compelling interest in the contemporary situation. He turns the tables on the other journal, by arguing that it is they who unwittingly advocate a revolutionary cataclysm, by their blindness to the facts of the situation. Marx's account of these facts is pregnant with many of the key ideas of his later writings. He argues that the position of the propertyless class in Germany at that time *vis-à-vis* the property-owning class is similar to that of the French middle class of 1789 *vis-à-vis* the nobility. We shall see in the course of this thesis how Marx develops such notions into the theory of class conflict, in which the concept of the propertyless proletariat will be central. In a third article, criticising recent laws against the gathering of wood by peasants on large landed estates, Marx attacks the basis of private property and the structure of society built on private interest.[20]

In this same period, Marx produced a *Critique of Hegel's Philosophy of the State*,[21] in which his debt to Feuerbach clearly emerges. He attacks Hegel's 'logical, pantheistic mysticism'.[22] To support his case, he runs systematically through paragraphs 261 to 313 of Hegel's work. He argues that Hegel correctly sees that the contemporary system is based on the division between *civil society*, in which men go about their day-to-day business, pursuing their own particular, material interests, and the *state*, which regards all men as equal, ignoring the inequality and narrowness which characterise their real lives. Where Hegel goes wrong, he claims, is in believing that the state is the reality, the active principle, and in some way gives rise to, activates, the existence of man in civil society.

Firstly, he attacks Hegel's methodology. In line with Feuerbach's ideas, he rejects Hegel's deduction of men's real lives from abstract, logical principles. He echoes Feuerbach directly when he accuses Hegel of making the state, which in fact is a predicate, a creature, of man, into a subject of which man thus becomes the mere predicate.[23] Hegel's system is repugnant because in it 'the sole concern is to rediscover the "Idea" pure and simple, the "logical Idea"'.[24]

Marx attacks Hegel's method not only because it works in the wrong direction, reversing subject and predicate, but also for another reason. When Hegel has deduced real life in civil society from the abstract idea of the state, he might as well,

Marx claims, have deduced it from the abstract idea of the solar system.[25] In other words, Marx does not want to replace Hegel's abstract idealist principle by *any* abstract principle. We must not only advert to material reality, but advert to the specific nature of each element of that reality. We must take real life in civil society exactly as we find it, and not try to impose on it some *a priori* schema, be it an idealist or a materialist schema. If we fail to do this, we shall differ from Hegel in being materialists, but remain like him in trying to reduce the intractability and raggedness of empirical reality to one tidy formula.

Secondly, Marx attacks Hegel on radical democratic grounds. He opposes Hegel's idea of the state, which presumes that: 'the people do not know what they want.'[26]

He rejects Hegel's claim that the organs of the state will create a really universal interest, and argues that they will be a bureaucracy independent of the wishes of the majority. Man in civil society, not abstract 'political man', is the *real* man, and so long as state and civil society remain apart, there can be no true democracy.

At this point, the break with the Bauer group had become irreversible, and these latter were launching attacks on all and sundry, even on those whom they might have regarded as moderate allies. Ruge thought of collaboration between his group and the French socialists (an idea which Feuerbach had advocated some time earlier). When members of the group arrived in Paris, he set about organising the joint Franco-German publication, *Deutsch-Französische Jahrbücher*. He got, in fact, little or no help from the French, and Feuerbach decided not to participate. Marx and Bakunin were involved with Ruge in the preparations. They had the advantage of at least a correspondence with Feuerbach, in which the four tried to systematise their basic opinions.[27]

Although Marx had already written to Ruge in January 1843 a letter expressing pessimism as to the possibility of achieving anything worthwhile in Germany, he had not in fact lost hope. Indeed, he rejected Ruge's pessimism as to the possibility of radical social revolution. Such a revolution, he declared, was not only necessary but possible.

AN OUTLINE OF MARX'S PRE-1848 WRITINGS

This brief outline of Marx's writings in the period before 1848 is intended to situate the *Essays and EPM* as a stage in the development of his ideas.

1841 Doctoral dissertation on the contrast between Democritus' and Epicurus' concepts of Nature. Marx declares his atheism, his belief in radical criticism, and his interest in the notions of freedom and activity.

1842–1843 (a) *Rheinische Zeitung*. Marx is moving away from the speculative criticism characteristic of the Bauer group. He is a radical democrat, and applies democratic principles to the political issues of the day. He also, in an article on communism, displays his concern with finding out the real facts of political life, and drawing his theories from them. We see an anticipation of his later developed theory of class conflict, and of the notion of the proletariat.

(b) *Critique of Hegel's Philosophy of the State*. Marx attacks Hegel for two reasons. (i) Under the influence of Feuerbach's anti-idealism and empiricism, he accuses Hegel of deducing reality from abstract principles, and is determined to lead criticism back to an encounter with material reality, which encounter will not be distorted by abstract aprioristic formulas. (ii) As a radical democrat, he cannot accept the dichotomy of state and civil society, and maintains that true freedom is impossible while this endures.

1844 (a) Two essays on the Jewish Question and one on Hegel's *Rechtsphilosophie*, all published in the *Deutsch-Französische Jahrbücher*. In these, Marx develops his criticism of the division of state and civil society, and in the process develops from a radical democratic to a socialist position. He elaborates the theory of class conflict and particularly the notion of the proletariat.

(b) *Economic and Philosophical Manuscripts*. Marx puts into practice his idea of empirically-based criticism, and builds a model of the working of the economy.

He applies humanist criteria to an assessment of economic life and of economics.

Finally, he makes the last and most systematic of his criticisms of Hegel. In this, he clearly displays the influence of Feuerbach's materialism, but also begins to go beyond

both Hegel and Feuerbach towards the philosophy of praxis.
(c) An article in the journal *Vorwärts!*, entitled 'Critical
Notes on "The King of Prussia and Social Reform"', in
which Marx attacks Ruge's pessimism as to the feasibility
of social revolution.

1845 *The Holy Family*, Marx's first work in collaboration with
Friedrich Engels. They finally declare their break with the
Bauer School, and give reasons for this break.

1846 *The German Ideology*, by Marx and Engels. Here the two
authors attack Bauer's speculative philosophy and Max
Stirner's 'abstract individualism'. There also emerges the
break with Feuerbach, which is clarified in the *Theses on
Feuerbach*, of the same period.

1847 *The Poverty of Philosophy*. In this work, Marx attacks the
a-historical methodology of Proudhon, and formalises the
theory that economic phenomena and categories are
historical products, in opposition to the economists' view
that they are the products of eternal and immutable laws.

1848 Marx and Engels produce what has since been regarded
as one of the classics of revolutionary socialism, the
Communist Manifesto.

THE SIGNIFICANCE OF THE ESSAYS AND EPM

As we have already noted in the *Preface*, not all commentators
agree as to the position and significance of the Paris writings
in Marx's total *oeuvre*. Berlin, for example, says that 'in Paris
(Marx) underwent his final intellectual transformation. At the
end of it he had arrived at a clear position personally and
politically: the remainder of his life was devoted to its development and practical realisation.'[28]

Similarly, Dupré argues that in the *EPM* 'all the results of
his previous studies are brought together in one powerful
synthesis to which he remains basically faithful in his later
work.'[29]

Althusser, on the other hand, would place well after the
Paris period that decisive 'break' which, he claims, cuts off
Marx's 'mature' works from those early writings not unen-
cumbered by Hegelian premises and terminology.[30] On this
interpretation, there would be little or no continuity between
the *Essays and EPM* and Marx's later thought. However,

whether we hold a 'continuity' or a 'break' theory, we must take account of the following radical developments in Marx's thought which occurred during the Paris period.

The Paris writings come at a crucial point in Marx's intellectual growth. They mark the end of his involvement with the pro-Feuerbach wing of the Young Hegelians. Equally, although he was already aware of Engels' work, (as we shall see in Chapter 3 below), this period comes just before the first joint product of what was to be a life-long partnership, *The Holy Family* of 1815.

(*a*) In the *Essays*, Marx develops from his radical democratic stance to a socialist stance. In the *Essays and EPM*, he elaborates the theory of class conflict, and in particular the notion of the proletarian revolution.

(*b*) In the *EPM*, he first turns his attention to an analysis of economic questions, which are to be the predominant interest of the remainder of his works.

(*c*) In the *Essays and EPM*, we see the seeds of the notion of praxis, which will be developed explicitly in the *Theses on Feuerbach* of the next year.

(*d*) The last section of the *EPM* contains a criticism of Hegel which is more profound and more systematic than anything which Marx had yet written, or was ever again to write, on this topic.

WORK ON THE ESSAYS AND EPM SO FAR

There are certain authors who have attempted to provide a balanced account of Marx's total output. Among these, Avineri[31] and Calvez[32] are of major importance. While both these authors take account of the *Essays and EPM*, the scope of their volumes does not allow of a complete exposition and analysis of these latter writings. As will emerge, I have made frequent use of their work. I do not regard this book as necessarily disagreeing with either Avineri or Calvez in what they have to say on the works with which we are concerned. The difference is rather one of scope, in that they are concerned to integrate *all* of Marx's work, in both the early and the later period, into one overall account. There are other authors who have concentrated more directly on the early period.

3

A pioneer in this latter task was H. P. Adams, whose book,[33] published in 1940 without the benefit of the many translations into English which are now available, represents a unique achievement in this field. As my references to him, particularly in Chapter 2 in regard to the development of Marx's theory of classes, will show, he makes important points which many subsequent commentators have overlooked. Again, I differ from Adams primarily in scope, in that he has given an admirable account of the pre-1848 writings, but could not go into the *Essays and EPM* in great depth. Delfgaauw's brief work[34] covers much of the same ground, but does not discuss each work so explicitly or so deeply as does Adams. Dupré[35] discusses the early development of Marx's philosophy and takes account of the *Essays and EPM*. Friedrich[36] lays especial emphasis on the economic aspect of Marx's early development, and also on the philosophical transition from Hegelianism. Bigo[37] discusses Marx's economic thought in general, and this book would differ from him mainly in scope, in that he does not go into the *Essays and EPM* at the same length as I have. Cottier[38] and Doyon[39] discuss Marx's thought on religion, paying special attention to the relevant section of the *Essays*, which will be discussed in Chapters 2 and 7 below. Livergood[40] gives a good short account of the concept of activity in Marx's thought, in which he deals with the early works. Rotenstreich[41] discusses Marx's early philosophy in general, although his account is based largely on the *Theses on Feuerbach*. McLellan's *Marx Before Marxism* gives a good account of Marx's early writings up to and including the *EPM*, but it is not the intention of his book to go into either the contents or the significance of the *Essays and EPM* in the detail in which this present work does.

CRITIQUE AND SPECIES-BEING

Throughout this introductory chapter, I have spoken of 'criticism' as a term applicable equally to the activity in which Marx engages, and to the activity of the philosophers whom he opposes. We have seen how Marx rejected both the speculative philosophy of the Bauer school, and the 'mysticism' of Hegel's system. Throughout the *Essays and EPM*, we shall observe Marx's attempt to formulate an acceptable alternative to these types of philosophy. This search will lead Marx to define criteria for a *critique* of society. We need not become involved in the complex semantic problem of defining 'critique' as distinct from 'criticism'. When I speak of Marx's search for a valid system of critique, I mean that he is looking for a system of criticism which will satisfy certain formal requirements. It will emerge that these formal requirements are that criticism should: (*a*) approach the facts as they are, rather than attempt to deduce reality from abstract, aprioristic notions; (*b*) interpret these facts in accordance with the correct philosophy of man, which latter will emerge also in the course of the *Essays and EPM*; and (*c*) issue in an effective practice which will transform reality so as to conform to the correct project for an alternative society which the critic will have arrived at by fulfilling conditions (*a*) and (*b*). Marx is engaged simultaneously in the search for the *facts* (as opposed to the 'mystifications' both of current established thought and of current forms of criticism) and in the search for a *correct critical attitude*. The two searches cannot be separated, because they are integral elements in the development of that correct understanding of and attitude to the world which will be formalised in the notion of *praxis*.

Denys Turner neatly summarises the elements which Marx regards as essential to a satisfactory critique: '"Critique" for Marx does not imply mere "criticism" in the usual sense of the word. A truly meaningful critique of society is . . . one which not merely recognises the true state of social relationships as they actually stand, but also actually realises new ones.'[42]

If critique is concerned to analyse the facts of current society, and to elaborate and implement a project for an alternative society, we may well ask: 'in terms of what does Marx analyse the present world, and propose an alternative world? As I have already suggested, it is possible to get a full understanding of Marx's philosophy of man only by a careful collation and analysis of the intimations scattered at random throughout the *Essays and EPM*. At this point, however, I shall give an outline sketch of the meaning of the term 'species-being' (*gattungswesen*), derived from Feuerbach, which is central to Marx's understanding of human nature and potentiality.

We have already seen that Marx, even before the Paris

period, had expressed interest in communist ideas, had attacked societies based on private property, and had used the concept of the proletariat in one of his articles.[43] It would thus be quite inaccurate to say that he had not yet displayed in his writings that emphasis on man's essential sociality which is almost synonymous with his name. Nevertheless the fact remains, as has been illustrated throughout this introductory chapter, that the central category of Marx's thought in the 1841–43 period is freedom rather than community, democracy rather than socialism. One of the chief points of interest in the *Essays and EPM* is the unfolding of Marx's notion of species-being, of man's essentially communal nature; it is in this sense that, as I have said, he develops in these writings from a radically democratic to a socialist perspective on man.

In Marx's writings, 'species-being' signifies not merely the *actuality* of man's living in society (his dependence on co-operation with others in industry, his experience in a world structured by a social language, and so forth), but also, and more importantly, his as yet unfilled *potentiality* for a kind of social living which is *really* social, where egoism and com-petitiveness are things of the past. The concept of species-being thus subverts, is a radical challenge to, established patterns of human activity and consciousness. But is it not merely an ideal of brotherhood, based on faith and love, but remote from reality? As we shall see in Chapter 3, Marx would deny this charge: he sees in current society an empirical verification of man's essential sociality, and in that society's deficiencies an indication of the real possibility and necessity of its more adequate fulfilment.

Furthermore, as we shall see in Chapter 4, the transformation of egoistic man into fully-realised species-being will be a real transformation of experience in the case of *each person*. It is not that we shall remain essentially unchanged 'atoms' of humanity which will happen to move in new orbits which are 'more social' in some external sense; on the contrary, our experience as persons will at one and the same time become, from our point of view, really human, liberated experience, and, from the point of view of our relation with other persons, really social experience; and this is necessarily so.

This points to the fact that, as will emerge in Chapter 7,

Marx's notion of species-being is, in intention at least, profoundly *personalist* rather than crudely collectivist. If, as I have argued, we do not become 'more social' in some empty, external sense of the word, this is because in communist society, where, Marx believes, our essential species-being will be realised, society will have ceased to be what he would call an 'empty, external abstraction' confronting the individual. We may summarise this notion of species-being, which underpins both Marx's critique of established social reality and his prescription of a more human alternative, with his own words to the effect that:

human emancipation will only be complete when the real, individual man has absorbed into himself the abstract citizen; when as an individual man, in his everyday life, in his work, and in his relationships, he has become a *species-being*; and when he has recognised and organised his own powers *(forces propres)* as *social* powers so that he no longer separates this social power from himself as *political* power. (B 31)

2

Critique of the Political Revolution in Terms of Human Emancipation

'Look at 'istory, Mr Gumbril, look at 'istory. First it's the French Revolution. They ask for political liberty. And they gets it. . . . And what's the result, Mr Gumbril? Nothing at all. Who's freer for political liberty? Not a soul, Mr Gumbril. . . . Political liberty's a swindle because a man doesn't spend his time being political. He spends it sleeping, eating, amusing himself a little and working —mostly working. When they'd got all the political liberty they wanted—or found they didn't want— they began to understand this. And so now it's all for the industrial revolution, Mr Gumbril.'

ALDOUS HUXLEY, *Antic Hay*

INTRODUCTION

The chief purpose of this chapter is to expound the writings in Bottomore up to the *EPM*. In view of the centrality of religion in the titles of the essays with which we are concerned, the title given to this chapter, with its emphasis on politics, may puzzle the reader. The title is, however, deliberately chosen in order to point to the fact that Marx is not primarily interested in the debate about religion: he neither affirms, nor spends much time in denying, the existence of a divine being. On the religious question, Marx presents the conclusion, that:

man makes religion; religion does not make man. . . . Religion is only the illusory sun about which man revolves so long as he does not revolve about himself. (B 43, 44)

For him, this is a conclusion which needs little or no supporting argument. Rather than debating the theological issues of the existence of God and the relations between different religious groups, we should turn our attention to eliminating those conditions which have *produced* religion in the first place:

the struggle against religion is, therefore, indirectly a struggle against that world whose spiritual aroma is religion. . . . The call (to men) to abandon their illusions about their conditions is a call to abandon a condition which requires illusions. (B 43-4, 44)

In Chapter 7 we shall consider some of the merits and weaknesses of Marx's thought on religion as such. For the moment what is of importance is to grasp that what Marx is concerned with here is the ability of the contemporary political society to emancipate men from those real defects in the real world of which religion is but a symptom:

thus the criticism of heaven is transformed into the criticism of earth, the criticism of religion into the criticism of law, and the criticism of theology into the criticism of politics. (B 44)

BRUNO BAUER, *Die Judenfrage*

The first of Marx's writings with which we are here concerned is a critical article on Bruno Bauer's *Die Judenfrage* (The Jewish Question).[44] There had been Jewish settlements in Germany since the fourth century A.D. Since that time, the Jews had become prominent as merchants and traders, so that their name became synonymous with these activities. In the fourteenth century, throughout Europe, they were subjected to repressive laws, and in France, Spain, Germany and Bohemia they suffered persecutions. It was not until the eighteenth century that their condition began to improve, with the passing of 'Edicts of Toleration'. Austria passed the first of these in 1782, followed by France in 1791, Holland in 1796 and Prussia in 1812. Despite this relaxation of persecution, however, the Jews still remained a class of outcasts, petty traders and artisans despised by all. The granting of civil rights to Jews had not yet become universal, and in practical terms they were still outcasts from the social and political life of the predominantly Christian states of the time. Bauer and Marx both write within the context of the demand of the Jews for the extension and real fulfilment of civil rights in Germany.[45]

As Marx is here discussing Bauer's opinions on this question, we should enter a *caveat* at this point. McLellan argues that Marx was a notoriously bad guide to the views of his opponents, often casting those views in the light which best suited his own polemic. He shows, for example, that there is a good case against Marx's charges of insufficient radicalism in Bauer.[46] As we are here concerned with obtaining a clear picture of Marx's *own* opinions, this point need not cause us too much trouble, so long as we are careful to recall that what we are getting here is 'Bauer *à la* Marx', and not necessarily a fair picture of Bauer himself.

Marx summarises Bauer's response to the Jews' demand for civil rights. This response, Marx tells us, is as follows. Firstly, Germans *as such* are not free, and the Jews should work for a free Germany rather than for their own sectional advance. Secondly, if they want the same status as the Christians, they are accepting the Christian state, in which neither Jew nor Christian can be free. Thirdly, neither this state nor the Jews, so long as each clings to a form of religious prejudice, are capable of being emancipated. Even if the Christian state granted the Jews a form of purely negative freedom, its very essence would be foreign and antipathetic to everything for which Judaism stands. Even if the Jew received such freedom, he would still, because of his religious prejudice, consider himself, and act as, a foreigner rather than a true member of such a state.

Thus, we are told, Bauer's solution is that the Christian state itself must be emancipated from Christianity before any progress is possible. Only then will it be meaningful to speak of freeing the Jews. The line of opposition between Marx and Bauer emerges when Marx characterises this response as a call for *political emancipation*.

Bauer demands, on the one hand, that the Jew should renounce Judaism, and in general that man should renounce religion, in order to be emancipated as a citizen. On the other hand, he considers, and this follows logically, that the political abolition of religion is the abolition of all religion. (B 7)

When Marx argues that Bauer envisages *political emancipation* of the *Christian state* from religion he means the following: that Bauer argues that the state which maintains Christianity as an official, established state religion should cease so to maintain it, and should relegate religion in importance from the public (*political*) sphere to the private sphere (that of *civil society*). Marx faults Bauer for having an uncritical attitude, in so far as he uses the idea of emancipation but fails to ask himself:

What kind of emancipation is involved? What are the essential conditions of the emancipation which is demanded? (B 7)

Marx assesses the *status quaestionis* of the Jewish Question in different countries. In Germany, which has not yet undergone the *political revolution* (that is, roughly, an equivalent of the French Revolution of 1789, which instituted the idea and the reality of the Rights of Man), the question is seen as entirely religious. In France, which Marx sees as halfway to being a fully developed political state, it is semi-religious, semi-political. Only in the United States, the one fully developed political state of the time, where the Rights of Man are fully guaranteed and there is no trace of the old Christian State, is it purely a political question, concerning the *political* rights of different groups within a society.

We get a further hint of Marx's criticisms of the notion of political revolution. He faults Bauer for granting that, even when political emancipation has removed religion from the public sphere, those who feel obliged still to practise religion should be allowed to do so in their private lives as members of civil society.

Human emancipation, which Marx opposes as a principle to political emancipation, is a rather shadowy idea as he presents it. In general we may safely say that the difference lies in that it is a more complete form than political emancipation. We shall see the ways in which political emancipation is, in Marx's eyes, incomplete, and we can begin to derive an idea of the meaning of human emancipation from seeing such arguments. The fault which Marx sees in political emancipation is that it is similar to the naïve behaviour of someone who dislikes me, and thinks that by not 'recognising' me he has actually 'cut me dead'. In the same way, the political revolution consists in a society's declaring that all the real differences which exist between men in their real lives will not be 'recognised' in the public sphere, where all men are 'equal', where 'universality' rather than particularity will be the principle.

The state abolishes, after its fashion, the distinctions established by *birth, social rank, education, occupation,* when it decrees that (these) are *non-political* distinctions. (B 12)

This points to a weakness in this public sphere itself. Marx tells us that this weakness arises from the fact that so long as men are unequal in their real day-to-day lives, so long as their real lives are characterised by particularity and divisions, the universality established within the political sphere can be no more than illusory, a 'theoretical' universality. As Lukàcs tells us, it is precisely on this point that: 'the vast difference between Hegel and the young Marx is to be observed.'[47] The fact that Marx is using the same *terms* (state and civil society) which are used in Hegel's *Rechtsphilosophie* should not blind us to the fact that Marx's idea of the state: 'has a quite different meaning from Hegel's, is, indeed, opposed to Hegel's conception of the state.'[48]

Both Hegel and Marx recognise the fact that society is divided into two spheres; where they differ is about the nature of the spheres. Hegel recognised the real differences between men in their real life in civil society, but held that the universality, the community, established in the public sphere was equally real, and could act as a principle of unity reconciling those real differences. Marx saw the public sphere as abstract and theoretical precisely because it is possible to speak of a *distinct* public sphere. So long as there is a distinction between state and civil society, between public and private spheres, the universality of the public sphere is no more than something set over and against the particularity of real life, something which in fact:

far from abolishing these effective differences, . . . only exists in so far as they are presupposed; it is conscious of being a political state and manifests its universality only in opposition to these elements. (B 12)

At this point Marx introduces the notion of *species-being* (*Gattungswesen*). Species-being implies, as we have seen in Chapter 1, a situation where man will have attained a *real* universality. This will mean that there will no longer be a distinction of public and private spheres either in society in the large or in the life and consciousness of each man. It will be the stage where each man has developed to the point of no longer being, or seeing himself as, an isolated egoistic individual whose welfare and growth are exclusive of those of other men. Thus we can see what Marx means when he says that the universality established in the public sphere by the political revolution is no more than an abstract, theoretical, unreal expression of man's species-being.

Because he has not yet become a real species-being, which he will become only when he has achieved full *human* emancipation, man in the present form of society lives in a sort of schizophrenia:

He lives in the political community, where he regards himself as a communal being, and in civil society where he acts simply as a private individual, treats other men as means, degrades himself to the role of a mere means, and becomes the plaything of alien powers. (B 13)

The universality and community to be gained in the political state can be gained only at the price of ceasing, within the public sphere, to be one's real self. Entering this sphere is rather like entering a mosque—one has to leave one's shoes outside! The fact that it is the difference of the two forms of emancipation, rather than the religious question *as such*, with which Marx is here concerned, is shown in his next argument.

The difference between the religious man and the citizen is the same as that between the shopkeeper and the citizen. . . . The contradiction in which the religious man finds himself with the political man is the same contradiction in which the bourgeois finds himself with the citizen, and the member of civil society with his political lion's skin. (B 14)

In other words, the contradiction between state and civil society is equally present in each form of the contradiction between man's theoretical universality in the public sphere and the various aspects of particularity and incompleteness which characterise real life in civil society, among which the existence of private religion is but one.

We should be gravely mistaken were we to conclude that Marx is here arguing *against* the political revolution and political emancipation. Far from arguing against them, he argues *beyond* them. In other words, the political revolution has what we may call a *double status*, in that it is an improvement over the past, but equally is incomplete in comparison with what will be possible in the future, namely full, human emancipation.

Political emancipation certainly represents a great progress. It is not, indeed, the final form of human emancipation, but it is the final form of human emancipation within the framework of the prevailing social order. (B 15)

The last phrase of this quotation must for the moment remain no more than a hint. The class theory which Marx will go on to develop will obviously fill the gap left by this open-ended and vague phrase. It would, however, be a mistake to claim that this theory was already developed to the point where we could read it directly into the present argument.

At this point we must advert briefly to an apparent paradox in Marx's argument. We have already seen something of his views on religion. These are most commonly, and indeed correctly, interpreted in the following manner. Because man is incomplete and partial in his actual life on earth, he attributes to an alien being outside himself certain powers which he fails to see are really his *own* powers which he has hitherto been unable to realise. Man is tempted to find:

in the fantastic reality of heaven . . . the semblance of himself—a non-human being—where he seeks and must seek his true reality. (B 43)

Religion is thus an 'encyclopaedic, compendious' (see B 43) expression of man's *total* alienated, inhuman condition. How then can it be that the religious man is in the same relation to the citizen as is the shopkeeper? Has religion suddenly become but one of a class of what we might call 'alienating factors', whereas it had seemed hitherto to be *the* expression of *all* alienation? The solution of this apparent paradox is of central importance for understanding Marx's ideas, and may be stated as follows. Man is a species-being, a being whose essence is to be social, to live in a society where the contradiction between individual and species will disappear, where each will have become, in company with all other men, all that man is capable of being but so far has been prevented from becoming. In any situation where man has not yet attained this full development, where real life is less than fully human, man will have to compensate by relating to some unreal, theoretical being outside himself. He will look to this being to find (*a*) the universality which is so glaringly absent from his own real life, and (*b*) all the potentialities of human nature which have so far been frustrated in the real life of real men.

In all of history up to the period in which Marx writes, this compensation has emerged as some form of religious consciousness, which is:

the fantastic realisation of the human being inasmuch as the human being possesses no true reality. (B 43)

Once, however, rational criticism has shown us that a being who is not only theoretical but *celestial* to boot is a little too much for modern man to stomach, then the downfall of religious thinking will begin. The decay of religion does not mean, however, that man automatically attains an earthly paradise. The practical problems of the real, terrestrial world are no whit nearer solution. Man lives still a life of particularity and egoism, he still fails to realise all his potentialities in himself. He thus requires a *new* illusory being, to provide that strange mixture of dominance and release which is needed to give theoretical fulfilment to the alienated mind.

Enter the developed political state. Here man finds, as hitherto in God, a being outside himself which will fulfil the requirements. His less-than-human real life is compensated for by the illusory universality of the public sphere which, as we have seen, simply does not 'recognise' within its own ambit the real defects of life in civil society. God is dead, long live the political state. Once this has happened, religion has obviously lost its real *raison d'être*, and is demoted from its throne. It now figures as simply *one* of the defects of real life in civil society, one among many of the signs of man's being less than human. It may still, as Bauer admits, provide solace to real man in his private existence; it has, however, lost its public role as the general expression and compensation of man's alienated way of life.

Between the two stages of this progression, the modern Christian state is the half-way point. It represents the temporary convergence of God-as-alien-being and the state-as-alien-being. It is, as it were, the gearbox through which the transference of power from one alien entity to another is effected. It is consequently caught in an irreconcilable tension between its loyalties to the celestial and the terrestrial:

the infamy of its profane ends (for which religion serves as a cloak) enter (*sic*) into an insoluble conflict with the probity of its religious consciousness (for which religion appears as the goal of the world). (B 19)

We can thus understand the serious meaning behind Marx's characteristically flamboyant and epigrammatic argument that the 'post-religious' democratic state is the fullest realisation of the religious, Christian state.

The democratic state, the real state, does not need religion for its political consummation. On the contrary, it can dispense with religion, because in this case the human core of religion is realised in a profane manner. (B 17)

Once more we see that Marx is less interested in 'religion' as such than in its 'human core'. This latter is the need for an alien being, which need will endure, although in different phenomenal forms, and even in increasingly *rational* phenomenal forms, until man *himself* has acquired a real universality and developed his own potentialities. The translation of the essence of religion into the democratic state can be observed even in the language of the latter:

creations of fantasy, dreams, the postulates of Christianity, the sovereignty of man—but of man as an alien being, distinguished from the real man—all these become in democracy the tangible and present reality, secular maxims. (B 20)

When we see what is really involved in this progression, and how little real life in civil society is improved thereby, we see how:

the emancipation of the state from religion is not the emancipation of the real man from religion. (B 21)

Thus we can see why Marx rejects the notion that the Jews should pursue political emancipation from religion, or, for that matter, from any of the factors in civil society which make man less than perfectly human. The next stage in the criticism of political emancipation comes when Marx says:

according to Bauer, man has to sacrifice the privilege of faith in order to acquire the general rights of man. Let us consider for a moment the so-called rights of man. (B 22)

Marx proceeds to characterise rights generally, before examining them specifically. In general, rights can be divided into two classes: (a) The rights of *participation*; these are the rights of each citizen as a member of the public sphere. They guarantee him political liberty and the exercise of his democratic functions, such as the franchise and so on. As we have already seen, the sphere to which these rights refer is essentially theoretical. Its being theoretical means precisely that it accepts, and indeed presupposes, the continuance of the real imperfections of civil society. It would thus be ludicrous to demand that the Jews should cease to be Jewish in order to achieve the rights of participation in a public sphere which is a mere empty abstraction relative to their real life in the real world. (b) The second class of rights are those of 'man' as distinct from the citizen, the rights of

a member of civil society, that is, of egoistic man, of man separated from other men and from the community. ... [The right to liberty] is a question of the liberty of man considered as an isolated monad, withdrawn into himself. ... Liberty as a right of man is not founded upon the relations between man and man, but rather upon the separation of man from man. ... The right of property . . . leads every man to see in other men, not the realisation, but rather the limitation of his own liberty. (B 24–5)

In general, therefore, these rights are precisely the *ne plus ultra* set up by the private sphere against the public sphere. They are the rights of man *not to be* a member of the community, they are the legislative foundation and protection of egoism and particularity. We can now understand more fully Marx's charges (a) that the public sphere is merely theoretical and (b) that it in fact *presupposes* the continued existence of the private sphere and its defects. This latter is shown by the fact that all the constitutions which have established the rights of man have seen the state (public sphere) as guaranteeing the existence of man in civil society (private sphere). The democratic state follows from, is a servant of, civil society, and thus is a merely theoretical sphere, having no reality in itself.

The sphere in which man functions as a species-being is degraded to a level below the sphere where he functions as a partial being, and . . . it is man as a bourgeois and not man as a citizen who is considered the *true* and *authentic* man. (B 26)

Marx, as we shall see throughout this thesis, sees man as a *historical* being, one who finds himself constantly at the crossroads between the encumbering defects of his present situation which has arisen through the events of his past, and the emerging possibility of a better way of life in the future which this present equally contains. It is thus entirely natural for Marx now to proceed to set the terms of his present discussion in historical perspective, to assess the evolution of the present situation in relation to its history, so that we may better understand what possibilities for a higher development of man that present offers.

This leads him to pay attention to the *political revolution*, through which the present has come to be what it is. This revolution was preceded by feudal society. In the feudal polity, man pursued many of the activities which we would now characterise as the activities of a member of civil society. In other words, he worked, set up a family, ate, drank, slept and so forth. These activities, however, were informed by a political character in the feudal polity. What Marx means by this argument is that feudal society consisted of a large number of small 'communities', the foundation of which was the relationship between lord and vassal. This relationship circumscribed all the activities of each member of the units of the feudal polity, so that there was no distinction either in his life or in his consciousness between a 'public' and a 'private' sphere. Albeit at a very primitive level in terms of human freedom and development, man lived a unified life but one of the indications of how primitive was this unity was the fact that each community was isolated from all the others. Ideas such as the universality and sovereignty of man as a member of society were meaningless, precisely because there was no 'society' as such, merely an aggregation of self-contained units.

The result of the impact of the political revolution on this polity was to shatter the units of which it was composed and this had the following consequences. (*a*) The notion of a society in the modern sense became meaningful, as signifying a very large number of people living under common rule in a geographical unit vastly greater than any single unit of the feudal polity. (*b*) The 'political' unified character of all aspects of life and activity in such units was shattered by the removal of the lord as the centre of power and integrating force of the lives of his vassals. (*c*) This form of life was replaced by a society (in the sense in which we define it in (*a*) above) which was divided between the public sphere of the *state* and the private sphere of *civil society*. (*d*) Life and activity in civil society lost the political character of life and activity in the feudal unit ruled by the lord. (*e*) The state was set up as something which claimed to restore a unified character to society. As we have seen, however, precisely because it is a sphere apart from the real life and activity to which it was supposed to give this character, the universality and community which the state elevated as principles are simply theoretical, abstract, unreal.

[The political revolution] set free the political spirit which had, so to speak, been dissolved, fragmented and lost in the various culs-de-sac of feudal society; it reassembled these scattered fragments; liberated the political spirit from its connexion with civil life, and made of it the community sphere, the general concern of the people, in principle independent of these particular elements of civil life. (B 29)

The relation of the terms of this analysis, and the meaning of the analysis itself, can best be clarified if we grasp that Marx is proposing a *dialectical* argument. A dialectic is concerned with two terms which are at first united, but in an external, almost superficial manner; these terms are then opposed, and finally reconciled in a more profound unity: the stages are those of immediate unity, mediation and mediated unity: 'the immediate is the simple and undifferentiated; it stands directly and immediately confronting us. . . . Mediation is the same as difference, division, distinction. . . . [Finally] the mediation and difference are merged in a new unity.'[49]

Let us see the two terms of the present argument as (*a*) man's

4

individual existence, his particularity as manifested in his real activity in the real world, and (*b*) his social nature, which manifests itself in community with, rather than in separation from, other men. Then we may say that these terms go through the phases of a dialectic. We have firstly the point where the two terms are united, but only 'immediately' united. The force of 'immediately' here is the same as that of 'primitive' as I have used this latter term. It signifies that the two terms are related simply because they have not yet developed in their own right. Neither of our two terms, man's particular existence and his sociality, has yet emerged to its full development. In the feudal polity they co-exist in a direct union, but only as temporarily sleeping volcanoes about to erupt in their own divergent directions. The eruption is brought about by the shattering impact of the political revolution on the feudal polity; this sets up the two terms as distinct and autonomous. Let (*a*) and (*b*) be the terms:

FEUDAL POLITY
Immediate unity of
(*a*) and (*b*) within
self-contained units

POLITICAL REVOLUTION
shatters this leading
to

MODERN POLITY $\Big\langle$ *(a) civil society*
(b) the state

What then of the synthesis, the phase which will integrate the two now autonomous terms of the dialectic in a developed, mediated unity in which they will be both fully developed and fully reconciled? This question itself gives us a fairly good clue as to what is intended, at least implicitly, by Marx's notion of species-being, the full development of which, through human emancipation, will constitute the required synthesis. We may derive a clearer idea of what all this implies, and round off the present discussion, in the concluding argument of this essay:

Human emancipation will only be complete when the real, individual man has absorbed into himself the abstract citizen; when as an individual man, in his everyday life, in his work, and in his relationships, he has become a *species-being*; and when he has recognised and organised his own powers (*forces propres*) as *social* powers so that he no longer separates this social power from himself as *political* power. (B 31)

BRUNO BAUER, *Die Fähigkeit*

Marx's next essay on the Jewish Question is a criticism of Bruno Bauer's *Die Fähigkeit der heutigen Juden und Christen frei zu Werden.*[50] Bauer writes within the context of the disintegration of official state Christianity, which we have already described. Within this context, he makes two demands on the Jews. Firstly, they must overcome that 'apartness' from the Christian way of life which makes them outcasts from the dominant culture. Secondly, however, they must embrace not Christianity in its established form, but 'Christianity in dissolution', and go the second step towards freedom, in company with the Christians themselves (see B 32). Marx objects to what he calls this

theological formulation of the question. For us, the question concerning the capacity of the Jew for emancipation is transformed into another question: What specific *social* element is it necessary to overcome in order to abolish Judaism? (B 34)

Although the argument in this essay is unusually epigrammatic and condensed even for Marx, we may discern its general theme. Because Bauer's formulation of the question is 'theoretical', he remains within the context of a *religious* controversy. Marx, on the other hand, wants to turn attention to the practical conditions in real life of which religion is but the reflection and complement. The problem of overcoming religion is a practical problem in the real world, not a 'religious' problem. Thus, *a fortiori*, the problem of overcoming Judaism is a problem of removing the social conditions which make Judaism possible. Marx claims that:

In emancipating itself from *huckstering* and *money*, and thus from real and practical Judaism, our age would emancipate itself. (B 34)

We should not see only the 'Sabbath Jew'. If we look at the

'everyday Jew' whose pattern of life is petty trading and the pursuit of money, we will see that in reality:

the Jews have emancipated themselves in so far as the Christians have become Jews. (B 35)

If Christians look not at the religious opposition between Judaism and their own creed, but at the actual life-pattern of the real world in which both live, they will see that they themselves have become Jews. This is because their own real life is infected with the values and attitudes which are the real basis of the Jewish creed. The extent to which these values and attitudes have permeated real life may be seen most clearly in North America, where even the preaching of the gospels has become an occupation, a business, like any other. Again, the Jewish cult of money and commerce has infected even sexual relations, so that 'woman is bartered away' (B 37).

Seen as different forms of the one essential defect, namely as forms of religion, and reduced to their real basis, their significance for man in the real world, Judaism and Christianity are related as practice to theory. It was only when the Christian vision of a transcendent paradise had completed man's alienation, his estrangement from his essential being in the real world, that Judaism could step in and further the de-humanisation of that real world in line with its own particular attitudes and forms of activity. Judaism is the principle of civil society, of narrow, practical, egoistic life, but 'civil society only reaches perfection in the *Christian* world' (B 38).

The force of 'Christian world' here is to be understood in the light of Marx's argument that the democratic state is the real fruition of Christianity. Only when the traditional Christian vision of man's fulfilment through God-as-alien-being has been translated into the modern situation where man is told that, despite the defects of civil society, he can achieve fulfilment through the state-as-alien-being, can the real defects of civil society develop freely. Only when Christianity in its new form (i.e., in the form of the state) has distracted us from the search for a humanised real world, can Judaism infect civil society with its principles of huckstering, petty-trading and the cult of money. In discussing this latter topic, Marx makes some points about the dominance of money over human relationships which we may disregard here, as they emerge at greater length and in more detail in the writings considered in Chapter 4.

While this essay is the shortest, it is also the most difficult to assess, of the writings which we have to consider. Before attempting to do so, we may review some of the problems of interpretation which it presents.

The first of these is Marx's explanation of Judaism in terms of its 'empirical essence' (see B 40), its real, worldly source.

Bauer regards the *ideal* and abstract essence of the Jew—his *religion* —as the *whole* of his nature. ... Let us not seek the secret of the Jew in his religion, but let us seek the secret of the religion in the real Jew. ... It is from its own entrails that civil society ceaselessly engenders the Jew. What was, in itself, the basis of the Jewish religion? Practical need, egoism. (B 33, 34, 36)

Marx does not make it at all clear how this 'empirical essence' 'produces' the religious consciousness of the Jew. If religion is, as Marx argues, in some sense a consolation for our sense of deficiency and narrowness in the real world, how is it that the Jew has a religion which, far from providing an (illusory) overcoming of his sins and failings, elevates them into fundamental principles? If it is an 'opium' (B 44), precisely what drugged condition does the Jew suffer, and what creates in him the need for such a condition? Furthermore, Marx's direct correlation of 'huckstering' and the cult of money with Jewish religious consciousness is at best questionable, particularly since Marx has to explain their prevalence in societies dominated by Christians as being the result of the Jews' having lain in wait over two thousand years while Christianity built up civilisation, and then infected civilisation with their own evil principles; one suspects Marx of stooping here to a prejudiced and necessarily circular argument. Neither Jewish history in general, nor Marx's indictment of human behaviour patterns in civil society under the post-Christian state in particular, would appear to bear out this unique correlation.

Thirdly, there arises the question of Marx's alleged anti-Semitism. Erich Fromm, speaking of this present essay, warns against misusing 'some critical remarks on the Jews, which were made polemically in a brilliant essay dealing with the problem of bourgeois emancipation, in order to make this fantastic charge against Marx.'[51] McLellan supports this claim by showing that Marx elsewhere, particularly in *The Holy Family* of 1845, vigorously supports the Jews, and regards the measure of their freedom as the measure of a society's degree of civilisation. He also points out that the word 'Judentum' means, as well as 'Judaism', also 'commerce', and says: 'it is this meaning which is uppermost in Marx's mind throughout the article. "Judaism" has very little religious, and still less racial, content for Marx and it would be little exaggeration to say that Marx's essay is an extended pun at Bauer's expense.'[52]

This may well be the case, but if so it is a pun based more on an analogy than on a mere equivocation between the two meanings of the word in question. When Marx tells us that the 'empirical essence' of Judentum/Judaism is Judentum/Commerce, there is every reason to believe that he means what he says. I would not argue that Marx is an anti-Semite, although I concede that, were I seeking so to prove, I would find much effective material in this essay. What can fairly be alleged against Marx on the strength of these pages is an inability, or an unwillingness, to grant to Judaism at least the same status as he attributes to other religions, little enough as some may think that to be. His attitude displays strains of post-Christian triumphalism, perhaps reflecting the fact that, as Kamenka says: 'he was not the first Jew to display *jüdischen Selbsthass*—Jewish self-hatred.'[53]

Is there, then, nothing at all of positive interest in this essay? I would not suggest this. While the essay does not break any essentially new ground in relation to the arguments we have already considered, it does highlight some aspects of Marx's thinking on the real significance of religious problems. Firstly there is a renewed warning against the error of seeing these problems only in their 'theological' form, and of thus ignoring the real problems in the real world to which they should direct our attention. Secondly, there is the related point that if we do grasp these problems correctly, we shall be led by our analysis to a transformation of that real world. Whatever prejudice and lack of scientific detachment he displays, Marx does develop his basic argument that religion in general is a symptom of an inhuman world.

CONTRIBUTION TO THE CRITIQUE OF HEGEL'S PHILOSOPHY OF RIGHT (INTRODUCTION)

The title of this essay, the last we shall consider in this chapter, is somewhat of a misnomer. This essay is far less directly concerned with Hegel than are, for example, the essay on Hegel cited in the introduction to this thesis, or the essay on Hegel's general philosophy which will be discussed in Chapter 5. The problem with which Marx is primarily dealing here is one which follows logically from the investigations and conclusions already examined in this present chapter. It also illustrates the importance of seeing the close connexion in Marx's thinking between the search for the facts and the search for a correct critical stance. What Marx tries to do in this essay is to outline the main features of the contemporary situation in Germany, and to find the critical stance which will (a) reflect these features fully and accurately, and (b) lead to an effective practice which will remove the real defects of the situation.

Having made some remarks about religion, to which we have already referred in this chapter, Marx proceeds to assess the position of Germany in relation to the history of other nations. He finds that the actual condition of Germany is unique. She has not yet had an equivalent of the French Revolution, but nevertheless has suffered from the reaction to that revolution, through the consolidation of reactionary regimes which followed the downfall of Napoleon I.

We have shared in the restorations of modern nations without ever sharing in their revolutions. (B 45)

In the 'stifling' political climate of Germany, the most important feature is an *ancien régime* which has not at all been affected by the challenge of democracy. It is 'the comedian of a world order whose real heroes are dead' (B 48). Does this mean that in every possible respect Germany lags behind the development of other nations? Not so, for paradoxically:

we Germans have lived our post-history in thought, in philosophy.

We are the philosophical contemporaries of the present day without being its historical contemporaries. (B 49)

Thus, for all its faults, modern German philosophy, consisting of the legacy of Hegel and the more or less valuable contributions of the post-Hegelians, is now discussing questions which not only are up to date with, but actually in some respects go beyond, the practical experience of the countries which have undergone the political revolution. German philosophy is not a mere reflex product of the concrete conditions of life in other countries, because:

our criticism stands at the centre of the problems of which the modern age says: *that is the question.* That which constitutes, for the advanced nations, a *practical* break with modern political conditions, is in Germany . . . virtually a *critical* break with their philosophical reflection. (B 50)

German philosophy has thus, in important respects, anticipated the 'practical break' which, be it noted, the politically more advanced nations have yet to achieve. Although this may be regarded as to Germany's credit, we should remember that Marx rejected 'solutions in thought' to what are in fact practical problems in the real world; thus it is not surprising that he regrets the fact that German philosophy is 'the only German history which is *al pari* with the official modern times' (B 50).

Obviously, the desideratum is a situation where German actuality not only will have caught up with the actuality of other nations, but will have attained to that even more developed actuality towards which some aspects of German philosophy already point. Marx distinguishes two main groups in German criticism according to their attitude to how this state of affairs is to be attained.

The first, or *Practical Party*, is obsessed with the contrast between German actuality and actuality elsewhere, and thus rejects all ideas, demanding some action for a change. Its mistake is to forget that the only source of effective action is in ideas which go beyond established actuality. Although it is rightly dissatisfied with the wonderful schemes of philosophers which leave the real world unchanged, it forgets that we would not know how to change the real world if we did not have ideas which in some way transcended the present state of affairs in that real world. 'In short, you cannot abolish philosophy without realising it' (B 50).

Precisely the opposite error is committed by the other, or *Theoretical Party*. These are so struck by the superiority of German ideas to anything to be found in German actuality, or for that matter in the actuality of any other nation, that they rest content with merely expounding those ideas. In so far as they take any notice of the real world at all, they appear to have some lordly assumption that it is enough to be a critical philosopher and that the real world will eventually realise its shortcomings and conform to the best ideas: 'it believed that it could realise philosophy without abolishing it' (B 51).

To understand what Marx means by 'abolishing' philosophy, we must advert to the meaning of the German verb *aufheben*, which figures centrally in Hegel, and which Marx employs here. As Bottomore points out, the word may be translated variously as 'annul', 'abolish', 'supersede' or 'transcend'.[54] What it certainly does not mean is 'remove absolutely, in every respect, from existence'. In the present case, we get an example of its complex but very important meaning. When Marx uses the term 'philosophy' here, he means philosophy as *a body of ideas which are not yet realised but which point beyond the present actuality to an alternative state of affairs which would be a higher development of the potentialities of man.*

Quite clearly, the implicit intention of any philosophy, on the above definition, is that it should cease to be what it at present is; that it should cease to be potential-but-not-actual, and become itself a new state of affairs, a new actuality. When this has happened, philosophy as defined above will have been 'abolished' under its aspect as potentiality, but only because it has been realised as an actuality. This is the force of Marx's *aufhebung* of philosophy. If we take account of what he says about the two parties, he wants us neither to reject philosophy in the name of mindless 'activity', nor to allow philosophy to rest content with a mere statement of what is possible. Thus philosophical criticism

does not remain within its own sphere, but leads on to *tasks* which can only be solved by means of *practical activity*. (B 52)

In other words, neither 'thought' nor 'activity' has any meaning for Marx in isolation; they must come together in a practice guided by thought, which neither of the two parties can achieve.

Marx now asks himself whether this desirable course of events can be achieved in Germany.

The question then arises: can Germany attain a practical activity *à la hauteur des principes*? . . . it is not enough that thought should seek to realise itself; reality must also strive towards thought. (B 52, 54)

In this argument we have a clear illustration of the link between the search for the facts and the search for a correct critical stance. No amount of philosophical ideas, we are told, will be of any use if they do not relate to what is really possible given the present state of affairs in the real world. In answering this question, Marx argues that there is hope for a genuine revolution in the state of affairs in Germany. This hope, paradoxically, derives from the very facts in that state of affairs which might make us expect his conclusion to be a pessimistic one. Precisely because Germany has had a reaction but no revolution, because: 'led by our shepherds, we have only once kept company with liberty, and that was on *the day of its interment*' (B 45), there is all the more reason to believe in the possibility of a revolution. The reason is that Germany has experienced all the sufferings of other nations, without even the mixed solace of having had a political revolution. Germany's decadence is, therefore, more profound than that of other nations, and thus requires a more profound revolution if it is to be shaken off at all. Elsewhere, the process of emancipation has got halfway, as it were, and then been 'defused' and lost its revolutionary force. In Germany, where there has been no safety valve, the pressure has built up for centuries, and cannot release itself at all without demolishing the whole structure which tries to contain it.

It is not *radical* revolution, *universal human emancipation*, which is a Utopian dream for Germany, but rather a partial *merely* political revolution which leaves the pillars of the building standing. (B 55)

The first question which arises is what Marx means by a partial or political, as opposed to a total or human revolution.

Partial revolution takes place, he says, wherever 'a determinate class undertakes, from its particular situation, a general emancipation of society' (B 55). The apparent paradox in this statement should alert us to the fact that for a successful revolution it is not enough that the revolutionary class should feel strongly about its particular wrongs. It must be able to convince the rest of society, with the exception of the current ruling class, that it represents a universal interest, that things will be better under the new rulers than under the old. For this, there is the critical minimum condition that the mass of society, who are neither the rulers nor the revolutionary class, must be disaffected within their present situation. They must have suffered enough at the hands of their rulers to afford the revolutionaries at least the negative support of non-opposition.

As we might expect, the defect of such revolutions is the result of their *partial* nature. They do not destroy the essential structure of rulers and ruled, but simply set new terms in this relationship. A complete revolution, which will remove the principle of dominance and class rule, can occur only when a class is formed which is

the dissolution of all classes, a sphere of society which has a universal character because its sufferings are universal, and which does not claim a *particular redress* because the wrong which is done to it is not a *particular* wrong but *wrong in general.* . . . This dissolution of society, as a particular class, is the *proletariat.* (B 58)

When industrial society has created a developed proletariat, in the manner we shall see in the next chapter, then there is the possibility of a revolution which will not result in the rule of a particular class, because it will be made by the proletariat, which is 'a class in civil society which is not a class of civil society, a class which is the dissolution of all classes' (B 58).

Thus the specific difference between the proletariat and all other classes is that the former are excluded from the life of their society. They are the negative face of that society, denied a share in its wealth and in its political life. Not being members of civil society, they can have no particular interest to establish through revolution. Since they make up the whole of society apart from the classes which at present enjoy political privilege, there is no class below them which they would oppress once

not true, neither theoretically, nor in practice.
How can the proletariat class, not be a class?

they seized power. It will be through the growth of this class that *reality* will, as Marx envisaged, strive towards the *thought* of a correct critical philosophy. Thus the argument that we saw about the practical and theoretical parties, to the effect that philosophy must be combined with action in the real world, is given a more precise meaning when Marx tells us that the proletariat will provide the material, real basis of the revolution which will be inspired by the correct philosophical ideas:

> philosophy is the head of this revolution, and the proletariat is its heart. Philosophy can be realised only by the abolition of the proletariat, and the proletariat can only be abolished by the realisation of philosophy. (B 59)

Our exposition has shown that Marx's main concern in the writings examined in this chapter was at the same time to find out what exactly were the facts of the contemporary German situation, and to establish the correct critical attitude. This latter would have two related functions. Firstly, unless we adopt the correct attitude, we will misformulate the questions, as do those critics who see religious questions as purely religious, and fail to see religion as a product of real defects in the real world. Secondly, this correct stance must be one which does not rest content with a mere philosophical statement of its criticism. It must lead to an action guided by philosophy, in which the ideas of the critic will be 'abolished' by being realised.

In his investigation of the facts of the situation, Marx, as we have seen, differs radically from Hegel's praise of the state. We should not, however, miss an important step in Marx's development beyond Hegel, which is all too easily missed. We would do so were we to argue that Marx rejects the Hegelian notion of the state because he has from the start a fully developed theory of classes, which theory makes him see the state as the instrument of a ruling class. The progression in his ideas is in fact almost the opposite of what this argument would suggest.

Hegel sees the state as a sphere of real universality, transcending and reconciling all the defects and the particularities of life in civil society. Marx asks whether this is really so and proceeds to demonstrate that it is not so, because so long as there remains a distinction of public and private spheres the former is inevitably merely 'theoretical'. We have noted that there is a hint of some of his later ideas in his remark about 'the framework of the prevailing social order' (B 15). This hint refers forward to the theory of classes, which we have just seen him develop. Only the proletariat can effect a revolution which will not move within but will destroy this prevailing social order; only the proletariat can achieve an emancipation which will be complete and human rather than partial and political. We stress the fact that the theory of classes emerges *after* the criticism of Hegel's notion of the state for a very important reason. Only when we realise that Marx develops his class theory after he has examined the claims of Hegel's notion of the state and found these claims to be invalid, will we realise that Marx is pushed to the analysis of the class structure because he believes it to be impossible to create a real community, a real universality of man, within the existing structure of society. Were we to assume that he started off with a theory of classes, we might well overlook the central importance of the idea of community and universality which lies behind this latter theory. We would be tempted to see Marx's analysis of society in terms of a crude distinction and opposition between capitalists and proletariat, and to note only the statements about class conflict which he makes, neglecting the fact that, as his idea of species-being shows, his central aim is the abolition of the class system and the creation of a developed human community.

In proposing this argument we should not make a naïve assumption about the chronological sequence of Marx's ideas. Indeed we have already noted Marx's early awareness of class conflict and of a propertyless class, in Chapter 1. I do not suggest that when he wrote the first word on the Jewish Question, Marx had no idea of the theory of classes, and that it hit him in a flash in the middle of the essay on Hegel's *Philosophy of Right*. What is important is the logical sequence of the ideas *as Marx presents them*, no matter when precisely he worked them out. What is of importance is that Marx makes criticisms of Hegel's notion of the state which are independent of his theory of classes. These criticisms hinge on the opposition

of the public and private spheres of society. He then proceeds
to formulate the idea of class dominance as the fundamental
condition which makes possible the persistence of this division
and the partial, political revolutions which occur within it.
Thus Marx rejects the Hegelian state not because he rejects
the idea of universality, of community, as such, but precisely
because he *values* that idea highly and finds that Hegel's state
cannot really achieve it. Marx's starting point in his inquiry
was much as Adams describes it: 'So far from seeing the
essence of society as a struggle between classes, he saw it as
the organism represented by the state. The separate interest of
a class he treated as an anomaly to be abolished in the name
of popular sovereignty and not yet as the ground of a conflict
to be developed until it found its dialectical conclusion.'[55]

Subsequently Marx comes to the point where this statement
from Avineri is a correct description of his position: 'Class
differentiation becomes for Marx the decisive factor in the
formation of the body politic, although on Hegel's assumption
property relations should be neutralised *vis-à-vis* the political
sphere.'[56]

The reason for stressing this aspect of Marx's development
is that otherwise we might ignore the ultimate objective of
his analysis, which is again well stated by Avineri: 'He still
retains the dialectical concept of a universal class, i.e. a partial
social stratum which is, however, an ideal subject of the
universal concept of the *Gemeinswesen*.'[57]

Another point about the development of Marx's ideas
examined in this chapter is made by Lukàcs, who sees the
essential transition as that from a radical democratic to a
socialist position.[58] It is only when he has examined the
claims of the political revolution, of the democratic state, and
found them unjustified, that he is prompted to proceed to a
more profound analysis of the conditions of modern political
life. This analysis culminates in the theory of classes and the
espousal, as a socialist, of the cause of the proletariat. Lukàcs
sees this movement as 'Marx's development of Jacobinism
beyond the horizons of the bourgeoisie.'[59]

Again, Marx does not relinquish the democratic ideal of
the liberty of man, but rather decides that if formulated only
as a democratic ideal, within the present structure of political

life, it can achieve no more than an incomplete, theoretical and ultimately contradictory expression. *because thought must be integrated w/ actuality.*

What of the development of Marx's approach to critique in these essays? I have repeatedly stressed that his ideas on this topic cannot validly be divorced from his investigation of the facts with which the critic should grapple. This is clearly shown in the arguments which we have seen him expound. What is the defect of political emancipation? That it can achieve only a *theoretical* community of men. What is the defect of incorrect critical approaches? That they rest content with a merely *theoretical* statement of their principles, and fail to affect the real world. Both the existing state of affairs and existing criticism thus manifest essentially the same defect. The first is a situation where man is incomplete, not yet a species-being; the second accepts this situation. Marx's solution to this problem, his search for a theory which issues in and informs an effective practice, is connected with his notion of praxis, to which we shall return in Chapter 6.

One last point about Marx's development in these essays. We have seen his rejection of a purely 'religious' formulation of religious problems, and more generally of purely theoretical formulation of practical problems in the real world. We have also seen a suggestion of what he believes is the essential nature of these practical problems, in his attempt in the essay on *Die Fähigkeit* to reduce religion to its *economic* basis. In the next chapter we shall see Marx proceed to analyse the economic life of his time, and throughout this thesis his growing conviction can be seen that we must tackle the problems of the economy if we are really to solve the various 'religious', 'political' and 'philosophical' problems of the world.

'In his early writings we see Marx proceeding from a critical examination of Hegelian philosophy to a direct study of the economic and political problems of modern society as they are represented in the works of the economists.'[60] In this context, we may question Lukàcs' argument that Marx, at the conclusion of the essays which we have just examined, and just before the *EPM*, saw political emancipation as being incomplete in that it was 'emancipation only in so far as it could extend within the capitalist economy'.[61] This argument reads Marx's *economic* analysis of the *EPM* period back into his 'pre-economic' analysis as we have seen it in this chapter. Marx has yet to discover the workings of the economy, he has yet to give an exact socio-economic reference to notions such as the proletariat. This he will begin to do in the writings examined in the next chapter.

3

Economic Analysis

> In demonstrating the laws of *laissez-faire* [the
> economists] had provided a critique of previous
> orders of society; but they had not provided an
> historical critique of capitalism itself. This latter
> remained to be done, unless capitalism was to be
> regarded as a stable and permanent order of
> nature or an unchanging final term of social
> development.
>
> MAURICE DOBB, in D. HOROWITZ, ed.,
> *Marx and Modern Economics*

INTRODUCTION

This chapter will contain an exposition and discussion of the
earlier section of the *EPM*; that is to say, it will cover the first
three sections of the *First Manuscript*, which appear under the
headings 'Wages of Labour', 'Profit of Capital' and 'Rent of
Land'.[62] The next chapter will cover the remainder of the
EPM, with the exception of the final essay on Hegel contained
therein. Lest that division, which is not made explicitly by
Marx himself, appear arbitrary and superfluous, I shall give
the reasons for making it.

One may easily be tempted to believe that what Marx does
to political economy is to reject it root and branch. We shall
find, however, that he often accepts the branches, and disagrees
only as to the root. In other words, we must not distort our
reading of these essays, or indeed Marx's other economic
writings, by expecting that at every point he will disagree with
the economists on questions of fact. Were we to take this
approach, we should constantly be puzzled by the number of
occasions on which his factual statements are, even to the
extent of direct quotation, the same as those of, for example,
Adam Smith. These we may call similarities at the *first level of
description*, in that they arise in the discussion of such questions
as what happens from day to day, as it were, in the economy,

what share of total wealth goes to the wage-earner, and so forth. The basic difference which arises between Marx and the economists emerges in their views, not on what are the 'first-level' facts, but on the context in which these facts are to be seen and evaluated. The difference of context can be put briefly by saying that Marx's context is historico-humanist. Marx insists on the historicity of economic phenomena,[63] and thus of the patterns of thought and behaviour associated with them. He argues that economic life is a product of the past activities of historical man, and not, as the economists openly or tacitly assumed, of autonomous a-human forces and 'laws'. Consequently, he argues that what is a historical product of men may legitimately be evaluated in the light of its *human value*, and, given the degree of freedom allowed to historical man by the process of history, can be replaced by a new situation which will accord more fully with the potentialities of human development. We shall be concerned in this chapter primarily with:

(*a*) Marx's analysis of factual economic questions, mainly of the respective shares in wealth of the factors of production, and

(*b*) an account of the relevance of his insistence on historicity, as this latter is the necessary transition from the discussion of immediate facts to the evaluation of these facts in the light of human values, the task which concerns him in the writings treated in the next chapter.

MARX BUILDS A MODEL

The most useful way of reading the writings covered by this chapter is to understand that Marx is attempting, for the first time, to do something which he achieved more fully and more sophisticatedly in his post-1848 writings; he is trying to build a model of the working of the economic society of early industrial capitalism. A useful description of the nature of a model is given by C. Wright Mills: 'a more or less systematic inventory of the elements to which we must pay attention if we are to understand something.'[64]

There is a point where the criteria of comprehensiveness and of simplicity will come into conflict in any model. If the former is upheld, the model will be as confusing as the original data, while the exclusive pursuit of simplicity will make the model so remote from the actual data as to be misleading. While these criteria should of course be kept in mind, we should not apply them so rigorously to the present writings as we would be justified in doing in the case, for example, of *Das Kapital*.[65] We are concerned here with Marx's first grappling with economic problems; the manuscripts lack system in many ways, and often give the impression that Marx is, as it were, 'thinking out loud', and recording the results on paper. It is, as I have said, useful to see Marx as building a model, but we are more concerned with the effort than the result, which latter is but a step on the long path to his more rigorous and developed ideas.

Preface to EPM (from *Third Manuscript*)

Marx tells us that the present writings are one of the preliminary sections of a vast work which he has projected, in which economics, law and other disciplines will be evaluated critically. When this is completed, a critique of Hegel's philosophy will be added as the coping stone. He also establishes his scientific credentials by an account of his researches in German, French and English (see B 63–5).

Wages of Labour

This section opens with the dogmatic assertion that

wages are determined by the bitter struggle between capitalist and worker. (B 69)

The significance of this short sentence, which contains the germs of much of Marx's leading ideas throughout the rest of his life, can be seen only in the context of contemporary economic orthodoxy, which it essentially challenges. In both the leading schools of thought at the time, Physiocracy and Classical Political Economy,[66] there was, despite their differences, a common element of determinism. Both schools thought that the economy operated in accordance with laws which were not amenable to human interference. One of the best instances of such determinism is the Classical school's *Iron Law of Wages*. This stated that any rise in wages would almost immediately induce a rise in population, with a conse-

quent fall in wages, which latter thus could never for any
significant time rise above the level of subsistence. In this
context we can see the (in every sense) revolutionary import
of Marx's setting human agency rather than 'invisible hands'
at the centre of economic life.

This point, of course, makes clear the difference of context
between Marx and orthodox economics. He then proceeds to
analyse the elements of this 'bitter struggle', and concludes
that the capitalist will always win, because (a) he can live
without the worker, who cannot however live without him,
(b) he can profit from combination, which is forbidden to
workers, and (c) he has diversified revenues, not being dependent on a sole source of income.

The absence of disagreement on points of fact is shown in
Marx's analysis of the level of wages in the various possible
economic climates; he quotes directly, without qualification or
correction, from Smith's account of this topic. Where societal
wealth is *falling*, wages will be the first to suffer. Wealth can
be *static* only where all productive outlets for capital invest-
ment have been exhausted; economic activity will thus decline,
there will be an 'over-supply' of workers, and their wage will
fall if they are lucky enough even to earn one. Marx accepts
that there is one situation—that of *rising* societal wealth—in
which wages will rise, but he argues that this will be achieved
only at the cost of more intensive and longer hours of labour.[67]
He concludes that the worker

has become a commodity, and he is fortunate if he can find a
buyer. (B 69–70)

Marx himself employs the methodology of the 'fact-context'
distinction in his clever use of Smith's own arguments to show
that:

since, however, according to Smith, a society is not happy in which
the majority suffers, and since the wealthiest state of society leads
to suffering for the majority, while the economic system (in general,
a society of private interests) leads to this wealthiest state, it follows
that social misery is the goal of the economy. (B 74)

Marx now proceeds to stand orthodox economics on its
head, saying that we shall

adopt entirely the viewpoint of the economist and compare in his terms the theoretical and practical claims of the workers. (B 74)

Marx gives a list of the inconsistencies of the assumption about the importance of labour which the economist makes, with a description of the actual condition of the labourer which he accepts in his formulations and in real life. Technically, we cannot help recognising that all wealth is due to the work of labour acting on inanimate matter. When it comes to the condition of life of the worker, however, the economist ignores this fact, maintaining that the workers cannot hope for more than the absolute minimum share in the total product. The bigger and better the product of his efforts, the worse becomes the labourer's poverty. A further contradiction exists where the introduction of 'labour-saving' devices has been simultaneous with an *increase* in both the intensity and the amount of work.

Although, according to the economists, the interest of the worker is never opposed to the interest of society, society is always and necessarily opposed to the interest of the worker. (B 75)

Marx follows up the section on wages with an attack on the prevalence of competition in economic affairs. Not only is there competition between worker and owner; even within the working class there is a struggle to get the employment which is always scarce, with the result that even where a few workers do benefit, the class must suffer.

He attacks the one-sidedness of economics, which treats the worker only as an economic agent and

does not deal with him in his free time, as a human being, but leaves this aspect to the criminal law, doctors, religion, statistical tables, politics and the work-house beadle. (B 76)

Marx gives us large selections from the works of Pecqueur and Schulz.[68] These raise the distinction between relative and absolute poverty, stress the connexion between industrialisation and rising crime rates, and depict the misery of men, women and even children in the factory system. A passage from Schulz (B 79) shows how the increase of industrial power has made possible the production of more wealth with less work, and yet hours of labour have actually increased over the years.

Lastly, we may note from this section a sentence from Marx himself which is an anticipation of some of the arguments which we shall see in greater detail in our next chapter:

in political economy *labour* appears only in the form of *acquisitive activity*. (B 77)

Profit of Capital

The opening passage of this section again clearly distinguishes the Marxian attitude from that of the economists. Marx refers both capital and labour to his historico-humanist context, and states that capital is merely 'stored-up labour' (B 85). The owner of capital possesses the power to hire and fire, to run the lives of others, not because of any personal qualities in himself, but because of his possession of wealth. Although wages are out of proportion both to the absolute amount of work done, and to any increase in length or intensity of work, at least there will be no wages without work; the capitalist's return is in no way linked to personal effort. In fact, the size of profits is related to the amount of inanimate capital which the owner is able to put to work for himself. This he does in pursuit of such profit, the number and welfare of his workers being a matter of total indifference to him. Profits can have any level up to that at which rent would disappear completely, and all wages would fall to the absolute minimum.

The capitalist makes a profit . . . first on the wages and secondly on the raw materials which he advances. (B 86)

At every successive stage of production more capital is being employed, and there is consequently a greater profit; this despite the fact that each new stage of wealth is due to an increased contribution of labour by the worker. Marx now turns to one of the most crucial topics of debate in his day, the opposition between competition and monopoly.

He accepts the notion that perfect competition would be a solution to many of the defects of monopoly, such as overpricing. He does not, however, see how such a state of affairs could be achieved in reality. The economist who opposes the two categories involved in this debate to each other is guilty of short-sightedness. In reality, competition and monopoly are

more closely related than many would care to accept. Competition is based on the assumption that each entrepreneur
will try with all possible means, fair and foul, to outdo his
rivals. This struggle will inevitably move in accordance with
what Marx calls *the laws of the movement of capital*. The essential
element of this movement is as follows:

Competition is only possible if capitals multiply and are held in
many hands. . . . [However] widespread accumulation inevitably
turns into accumulation by a few. . . . If . . . large capital is opposed
by small capitals with small profits, as happens under the assumed
conditions of intense competition, it completely crushes them.
(B 93)

The reason for the emergence of a number of dominant
monopolists as the inevitable result of competition, despite the
alleged opposition between the two, lies in what are called
the *economies of large-scale production*.[69] We need not repeat
Marx's list here; the essence of these economies is that they
are all instances of costs which do not rise in direct proportion
to any given rise in the scale of output. Once a mixture of skill,
ruthlessness and chance has given the first break to a few
entrepreneurs, their success is rendered cumulative by these
advantages, just as the decline and eventual fall of their less
successful rivals is made cumulative and inevitable.

Concentration of capital in a few hands is a necessary consequence
when capitals are left free to follow their natural course. (B 91)

We must give attention to one of the advantages which
Marx lists, because, as we shall see, it contains the germs of
one of the central conceptions of his later economic theories.
He accepts the distinction, commonplace in Classical economics, between *fixed* capital, embodied in machinery, and
circulating capital which the producer pays out to cover the
wages and the raw materials involved in production. It is the
latter, says Marx, which gives rise to profits, because the
capital fixed in machinery cannot increase in value.

It will be seen at once that the relation between fixed and circulating capital is much more favourable in the case of the large
capitalist than in that of the smaller capitalist. The additional
fixed capital required by a great banker, compared with a very
small one, is insignificant. (B 94)

Marx repeats his attack on the anarchy of free competition, which we have already noted in the section on wages. There is a complete lack of co-ordination between demand and supply, and the blind law of profit prevails over the needs of people. Once more political economy is indicted for its narrowness of outlook, regarding nations as vast factories, and men only as machines for producing and consuming wealth. We see once more that Marx does not dispute the 'first-level' facts, nor the existence of 'economic laws'; what he does deny is the necessity for them to 'rule the world blindly' (B 98).

Rent of Land

It is essential to grasp the politico-economic context in which Marx's discussion of the land question is situated. This context is the result of two major historical events in the centuries preceding his life-time. The first of these was the movement in which, over a number of centuries, the common pasturage of early feudal days had been enclosed into the large landed estates characteristic of the developed feudal polity. This movement represents the rise and consolidation of large feudal landed property. The second event was the impact of the rise of industry on the nature and importance of agricultural production in these large landed estates. With this development of industry, there arose a conflict of interest which is best illustrated by the controversy preceding the abolition of the British Corn Laws in 1846. These laws prohibited importation of foreign foodstuffs until the price had reached a certain level in the domestic market. This meant that domestic suppliers could reap handsome profits from a shortage, with no fear of competition until the shortage had achieved the proportions of crisis. The manufacturers had an opposite vested interest, desiring a ready supply of cheap food so that wages could be kept low. The repeal represents the victory of the latter, whose case was strongly advocated by the founders of Classical political economy.[70] The basic opposition involved in this controversy was to be a reality for every industrialising country, although it had reached its highest form in Britain. Marx's own comment on the German situation in an earlier essay shows that he was aware of the particular form of the debate in Britain; our example is thus relevant.[71]

The Classical economists, following Smith, maintained that rent was an unearned income, since there was no cost of production. Marx accepts this analysis, showing, indeed, much of these economists' own polemical bitterness against the landowning class, who

love to reap where they never sowed, and demand a rent even for the natural product of the land. (B 103)

Marx recalls his own analysis of the genesis of wages, and generalises this analysis in a statement about economic life as such:

The rent of land is established by the struggle between tenant and landlord. In all political economy we find that the hostile opposition of interests, struggle and warfare, are recognised as the basis of social organisation. (B 105)

The landlord will leave the tenant only the minimum share of the total product which will suffice for the latter to pay his costs and keep himself in business. Marx clearly accepts much of the economists' 'anti-land' bias, arguing that the landowner exploits every advance of society by levying rent on the consequent increase in the value of his land.

There are close (logical) similarities between Marx's treatment of the determination of wages in the worker/owner struggle, and his treatment of the genesis of rent in the tenant/owner struggle. The landowner has many of the advantages earlier attributed to the capitalist. Equally, the large and small landowners stand in a relation similar to that of large and small capitalists. But there is a difference of status between the land and industry. In the movement of capital to which we have already referred, the latter is due to engulf the former, the landowner to become either a capitalist or a bankrupt:

the final result is . . . the abolition of the distinction between capitalist and landowner, so that broadly speaking there remain only two classes in the population, the working class and the capitalist class. (B 113)

Marx now proceeds to a more general analysis of the movement of the economy from feudalism to industrialism. We have already noted in Chapter 2 his analysis of the impact of the

political revolution on the feudal polity; there are many
parallels between that analysis and the present discussion of
the impact of the economic revolution on the feudal economy.
This impact is one which disrupts the primitive, immediate
simplicity of the feudal system. Although feudal landed
property is in fact as much a form of private property as are
those relations of property which succeed it, it is disguised by
the political system of lordship.

There is an appearance of a more intimate connexion between the
owner and the land than is the case in the possession of mere
wealth. . . . [The] relation [of the lord] to [his labourers] is . . .
directly political and has even an agreeable side. (B 114)

The essential feature of the economic revolution is that it
represents the emergence of capital, of dynamic wealth which
constantly accumulates. The rise of industry shatters the bonds
of the feudal economy. Land ownership is revealed as a form
of private property, the relationship of owner to worker is
revealed as one of undisguised exploitation, and the element
of personal relationship which provided the 'political colouring'
of feudalism is shattered. This is all part of the movement
towards a society polarised between two large classes, which
Marx has already prophesied, and also towards the antagonism
of *abstract labour* and *abstract capital*, of which we shall see more
in the next chapter.

Marx discusses one of the burning questions of the day, that
of the division of landed property. Two solutions have so far
been offered to the problem involved here. One side has
called for a return to the feudal land system of great estates,
the other has called for the further sub-division of these estates.
Marx argues that the proponents of these two cases, the
landed and the industrial classes respectively, are both incapable of justifying themselves, if the question is seen clearly and
reduced to its essential elements. The first solution would not,
as its proponents claim, remove the defects of sub-division
while allowing for the benefits of large-scale cultivation; it
would rather be a relapse into a primitive, sluggish monopoly.
The other solution would merely generalise the system of
private property, and would eventually lead to a new form of
monopoly, for private property and competition in land, just

as in industry, inevitably lead to accumulation and monopoly.

Marx is here performing a logical operation which gives us a further insight into his critical method. Exactly as he reduced Judaism and Christianity, which their proponents and the critics saw as opposed and exclusive, to their common membership of the category *religion*, so he reduces both of these allegedly opposite solutions to the element common to both of them, namely, that they are both forms of *private property*. As in the case of the religious debate, we see that the answer to the problem is not to accept one side to the exclusion of the other, but to remove the essential defect of which they are both manifestations; in this case, to destroy the very principle of private property, with its inevitable concomitants of competition and accumulative monopoly. The way to do this, Marx argues, is by association. Under this system the land would be owned by all, who would work it co-operatively for the benefit of all. This would realise at the same time the advantages both of equality and of large-scale cultivation, without the defects of either. Man would then relate to the land rationally,

instead of through serfdom, overlordship, and a foolish mystique of property. (B 116)

Marx demolishes the special pleading of both the landed and the industrial classes, and shows that they are much more at one in their acceptance of the idea of private property, in their pursuit of profit and accumulation, and in other respects, than they would be ready to admit. Despite the actual differences between these two classes, they are both the representatives of forms of economic life which must be totally replaced, and this is far more important than the smokescreen of their polemics. So close, indeed, have the two become, that

as we have seen in England, large landed property has cast off its feudal character and has taken on an industrial character to the extent that it wants to make as much money as possible. (B 118)

Just as landed property had to suffer from both monopoly and competition, before Marx's 'association' would appear as the only possible solution,

so also industry had to ruin itself both in the form of monopoly and

in the form of competition, in order to arrive at faith in man.
(B 119)

CHARACTERISTICS OF THE MODEL

Although, as was earlier pointed out, the criteria for a
valid model should not be applied too rigorously in the present
case, we may say that Marx has given us an inventory of what
he considers necessary for an understanding of the economy of
early industrial capitalism. I shall briefly outline the structure
of this model, and its chief dynamic factors.

We have an economy of two sectors, land and industry.
Within each there is a division, in that one group (the owners)
hold economic power and another (the workers) depend on
this group. The division of wealth between these two groups
in each sector is the product of a struggle in which the former,
having the power, set the reward of the latter. The former
group's income is unrelated to personal effort; the workers' is
totally dependent upon, but does not increase in proportion
to, their work.

The basic assumption of this model is the principle of
private property; the resultant competition leads inevitably,
despite the beliefs and rationalisations of the economists, to
accumulation and monopoly, because such an economy must
be a victim of the movement of capital. This latter is the most
important long-run trend of the system, because it means that
eventually the land sector will be subsumed under the rise of
the industrial sector. This means that the economy will no
longer contain two internally divided sectors, but will eventually be polarised into the two classes: capitalists and
proletariat.

The centrality of private property and competition means
that the whole economy is based on an internal contradiction.
Before polarisation, we find that the interests of owners and
workers in each sector are diametrically opposed; moreover
the interests of individual members of these sub-groups are
also opposed to one another, because the owners choose, and
the workers are forced, to compete among themselves. After
polarisation we have two opposing classes of workers and
owners, with still the division of interests within each class as
well as the class opposition. The only solution to the principle

of private property is to abolish it and organise the economy along the lines of association and co-operation, thus overcoming the situation where

the interest which an individual has in society is in exactly inverse proportion to the interest which society has in him. (B 109)

The main defect of the system based on private property and competition, from the viewpoint of economic efficiency, is that it is a totally irrational system:

The producer does not know what are the needs and resources, the demand and supply . . . Supply knows nothing of the demand, and demand knows nothing of the supply. (B 98)[72]

One of the results of this irrational system is the cycle of booms and slumps, the symptoms of an economy which is based on the narrow calculations and competition of the producers rather than on the fulfilment of human need. The extent of such need is amply proved by the existence of the dire poverty of the worker in face of the immense wealth which his efforts have produced.

As a result of . . . accumulation the same volume of industry produces a *greater quantity of products* which leads to overproduction and culminates either in putting a great part of the workers out of work or in reducing their wages to the most wretched minimum. (B 73)

THE MODEL AS A STAGE IN MARX'S ECONOMIC THOUGHT

Our concern here is not primarily with Marx as an economic thinker; still less, therefore, are we concerned with the economics of the *later* Marx. It will be useful, however, to consider the relation of the writings which we have just examined to Marx's later theories in the same field.

Much light has been thrown on this relatively under-discussed topic in an article by Martin Nicolaus.[73] The subject of this article is Marx's *Grundrisse der Kritik der Politischen Ökonomie (Rohentwurf)*[74] which lies in the period between the *EPM* and *Das Kapital*.[75] Nicolaus makes an impressive case for his thesis that 'between the mature Marx and the young Marx the *Grundrisse* is the missing link.'[76] He suggests that the chief difference between the *EPM* and the *Grundrisse* is that 'while Marx's earlier economic writings had centred around the movement of *competition*, in the *Grundrisse* he analyses systematically, and for the first time in his work, the economics of *production*.'[77]

In other words, there is what Nicolaus calls a 'qualitative break-through'[78] between the two works. We have seen the extent to which, in the *EPM*, Marx is concerned with the market, and with competition; in the later writings he moves to a study of what he himself would regard as the deeper level, that of production, over which the movements of competition and the market would henceforth be merely so many veils. The chief fruit of this advance is the theory of Surplus Value.[79] This theory rests on the distinction between the *market price of labour* and the *value of labour power*. The former is the subsistence wage which the worker receives; the latter is the wealth-producing capacity of his work, which gives to the producer a far greater amount of revenue than the amount expended in wages. It is from this difference that the producer derives his profit, or surplus value. The capital which covers all the aspects of production except labour is constant capital, as it makes no surplus; the remainder, which hires the labourers, is variable capital. The greater the proportion of the latter to the former, the higher the level of profit to the owner.

I have explained this theory in some detail, in order to give one important instance of the development from the *EPM* to the *Grundrisse* in this area of thought, rather than reproducing the whole list of comparisons and contrasts. The development towards the full theory of surplus-value exploitation is as follows.

In the writings which have just been analysed we get a strong impression that the capitalist 'exploits' the worker. We are told[80] that the greater the share of human effort involved in any product, the greater the profit of the owner, the less the reward to the worker. The problem is that we cannot be quite clear as to exactly how this happens. This puzzle is clearly stated by Dobb: 'why, even though there might exist a difference between the expenses of production and the value of the product, should the difference accrue to the capitalist and his partners rather than to anyone else?'[81]

We know that a lot of wealth is created by the worker, and that the capitalist and not the worker benefits. But, given that the wage, however unjust, is the market value of the work, how can we evolve a framework of ideas which will show (*a*) *how* the owner appropriates the wealth and (*b*) how this wealth is really the product of the worker, who *appears* to have been given his legal, if not moral, share in it?

The precise conceptual advance made between the two works, which gives us Marx's answer to this puzzle, has not been fully recognised by the commentators, including Nicolaus himself, although Bigo does hint at it.[82] In *EPM* Marx employs the Classical distinction between *fixed* and *circulating* capital, whereas in the *Grundrisse* he uses the distinction between the *constant* and *variable* capital. The crucial point here is that circulating capital covers both labour and materials, whereas variable capital covers only the hire of labour. Although Marx had already seen the distinction between active human labour and passive inanimate matter as the vital clue, he was still, at the *EPM* stage, working within categories which did not allow him to express this distinction. It was only when, in the *Grundrisse*, he made the distinction between the capital which employs matter and that which employs men, that he could give a precise formulation of the process of exploitation of surplus value. Two points are to be noted here. Firstly, the importance of the conceptual advance lies mainly in that it enables Marx to state clearly something which he sees but cannot fully express in *EPM*—the uniqueness of the role of the human agent as distinct from that of mere matter. Secondly, this analysis confirms Nicolaus' thesis, for it is only when Marx sees the fundamental differences between the market mechanism, in which everyone appears to benefit equally from an exchange of equivalents, and the production process, in which exploitation occurs, that he can really make his precise critique of the capitalist economy.

THE EPM AND ENGELS

In the Introduction to the *EPM*, Marx refers to an essay by Engels as one of the few important works on political economy in German. This essay, 'Umrisse zu einer Kritik der National-ökonomie'[83] was written very shortly before the *EPM*, and it is

of interest briefly to compare the two, as they come just before
the first collaboration of the two authors in *The Holy Family*
of 1845.

Engels' work is more clearly a technical critique of political
economy as such than is Marx's longer and more wide-ranging
document. This does not mean that he does not refer to many
of the points which we see Marx refer to concerning what in
the next chapter we call the external critique of economics in
terms of humanist criteria; he often does so, indeed, with great
force. The fact remains, however, that Engels is more closely
confined to a technical and methodological confrontation with
technical economic theories than is Marx. The underlying
vision of Engels' essay is of a society which has produced great
wealth, and has the capacity to produce vastly greater wealth,
a society whose advances are *social* in the sense that they arise
from, and properly pertain to, men working as an active
community. The problem is, however, that this wealth has
arisen in the framework of economic organisation based on
private property, so that the economy, and similarly the ideas
of economists, are caught up in a profound series of contradictions between the social nature and purpose of wealth and
the private-property relationship which still persists. Engels
stresses, as we have seen Marx stress, the irrationality of such
a situation, and the fact that private property and competition
lead to monopoly rather than being opposed to it. The 'liberal
economists'

have destroyed small monopolies so that private property—the one
great basic monopoly—may function more freely.[84]

The contradictions of the economists are shown clearly in
their attempt to solve the problem of value—of how articles
are given a market price. On the one hand we have the
Classical school, with their insistence on costs of production as
the determinant; on the other, the French economists stress
the role of demand. This shows how they are unable to reconcile
the processes of the market and of production:

Let us try to clear up the confusion. The value of an article includes
both the factors which the contending economists have so rudely
and so unsuccessfully attempted to separate.[85]

In his sections on rent and labour and elsewhere, Engels

drives home the point of the irrationality of a system of social production based on private interest.

So long as private property exists everything is regulated by competition. . . . If private property is abandoned all these unnatural divisions disappear. . . . The difference between capital and labour [disappears].[86]

Engels devotes much more attention to the Malthusian theory of population, which is in its essence similar to the Iron Law of Wages, which we already outlined, than does Marx. He argues that it is merely a rationalisation, a stop-gap, invented by the economists to make them feel happy about a society which has the power to feed all its population and more besides, but which allows the majority to suffer poverty and even death.

Economists *cannot afford* to accept the truth. They cannot afford to admit that the contradiction of wealth and poverty is simply the consequence of competition.[87]

There are many other points of interest in this essay. Engels distinguishes between 'merely natural' processes, and those controlled by human intelligence for the benefit of man.[88] He represents economic science and industrial society as being real advances over the ideas and realities which preceded them, however inferior to the possible alternatives they may now appear.[89] We shall conclude the discussion of his work by giving what we consider to be the main theme of the whole.

Throughout all the discussions of various topics runs Engels' objection to a society where

the interests of society and the interests of the individual are in complete opposition. . . . Private property has turned man into a commodity. . . . So monopoly and competition must be abolished by introducing a new principle which will embrace both of them.[90]

That Marx must either have got many ideas, and even expressions, from his reading of this essay, or else been confirmed by it in many of the notions which had already occurred to him, will be clear even from our short discussion. We need not attempt to measure the extent of this influence, except to note that the minds of the two men at this stage seem already to have been in that unconscious empathy which made possible the famous collaboration that was so soon to begin. The chief difference between the two lies in the aspects of Marx's thought which we shall consider in the next chapter. Marx combines his methodological and technical assessment of economic science with a critique of that science in terms of human criteria based on a framework of anthropological and 'philosophical' notions. Although Engels is at times strikingly aware of the need for such a critique, and even at times contributes to it in this essay, he does not do so as comprehensively or as effectively as we shall see does Marx.

THE ECONOMY AS HISTORICAL TOTALITY

Marx insists frequently that his critique begins not from some arbitrary point of reference, but from political economy itself:

Let us confine ourselves to the propositions of political economy itself. ... Let us now adopt entirely the viewpoint of the economist and compare in his terms the theoretical and practical claims of the workers. (B 110, 74)

Throughout his critique, as I have already suggested in the Introduction to this chapter, Marx accepts many passages from the political economists as being accurate descriptions of contemporary economic reality. What he is telling us here, however, is that the economists are involved in insoluble contradictions between their theoretical postulate of the primacy of labour, and the actual position of labour as revealed in those descriptions. This is the first of the many defects which Marx alleges in the economists' position.

Their second deficiency is their failure to grasp economic reality as a complex totality of interacting forces. They isolate, as we have seen, categories such as 'competition' and 'monopoly' and treat them as opposed, when in fact, being different forms of private property, they are destined to become one as competition drives out the small capitalist in favour of the monopolist. The economists fail to see the interaction of:

private property, acquisitiveness, the separation of labour, capital and land, exchange and competition, value and the devaluation of man, monopoly and competition. (B 121)

This is a point which Marx will bring out in much greater

detail in *The Poverty of Philosophy* (1847), where he condemns Proudhon for isolating, as apparently autonomous, elements of the economic and social complex which are in fact closely intertwined. Because the economists fail to grasp economic life as a totality they are incapable of grasping it as a *historical* totality. Their failure to grasp interaction is intimately related to their failure to grasp the direction in which the economy is moving as a result of that interaction. It is this latter failure which leads them to hypostatise as eternal and immutable correlations and 'laws' which in fact hold only of a given and historically relative situation.

Marx goes on to make a criticism which appears directly to contradict what has just been said. He faults the economists for putting forward the conditions of contemporary economic life as 'eternal and accidental'. Surely he cannot accuse them of regarding economic conditions as both immutable and accidental, both intrinsically necessary and fortuitous, at one and the same time? Marx does, in fact, make these charges, and they are compatible and at the same time fundamental in his argument. The two charges point to the fact that the economists regard the conditions of economic life as given, as independent of man, totally prior and superior to human agency and interference. They thus present economic reality as eternal and immutable. When the question of how this economic reality came into being arises, the economist can give no answer in terms of social evolution or human agency, from which he has explicitly divorced it. When faced with the division of labour and capital, for example,

how these two factors, as two persons, spring at each other's throats is for the economist a *fortuitous* occurrence, which, therefore, requires only to be explained by external circumstances. (B 175)

Thus the economists posit economic reality as *fortuitous* in that it cannot be explained, and *necessary* in that it cannot be altered, by human activity. Marx rejects both of these claims. He argues that the economists fail to see

the extent to which these external and apparently accidental conditions are simply the expression of a necessary development. (B 120)

Equally, in the *Notes on James Mill* of 1844, he argues for our freedom with regard to the anthropological strait-jacket of *homo oeconomicus*, that:

economics rigidifies the alienated form of social intercourse, as the essential, original form that corresponds to man's nature.[91]

In discussing this aspect of Marx's thought, Delfgaauw falls into a serious error. He says that 'among the other things he owed to [the English] economists, Marx owed the idea that economic development is determined—that it is a kind of natural phenomenon which can be expressed in terms of laws.'[92]

There can be no doubt that there are strong strains of determinism in Marx's system of thought; the passage already quoted about a '*necessary* development' clearly raises this issue, which we shall discuss in its own right in Chapter 6. Delfgaauw's formulation nevertheless obscures the vital point that, however determinist he himself might be in some relevant sense, Marx is arguing strongly *against* the a-historical determinism of the classical economists. This argument is not inconsistent with the fact that he often agreed with the economists that the economy operates in accordance with laws; he could accept this, and still question whether those laws were of such a nature as to be beyond human interference. Dupré puts this point well, and makes an interesting observation on the influence on Marx's thinking of Engels' essay: 'from Engels' article he now learnt that the laws which rule an economic system escape all human control. *As soon as a particular system is adopted*, man has no further control over its operation.'[93]

All of Marx's indictments of the established economists are underpinned by his most fundamental charge, that they have no historical sense, that they fail to grasp the economy as a product of human action in history which is open to change in the process of history. This point is vital, as it is the crucial transition-point from the element of technical discussion and analysis in the essays treated in this chapter to the critique of economics in terms of humanist criteria which we shall review in the next. Marcuse puts this point well when he describes Marx's rejection of the type of economics which we have seen him attacking, in favour of 'the interpretation that economic relations are existential relations between men.'[94]

In other words, it is only when Marx has (*a*) built a model of how the contemporary economy works and (*b*) shown how this contemporary economy, and the ideas used to describe it in established economics, are both products of man's action in history, that he has a sure basis for the evaluation of the modern economy in terms of its ability to achieve the full development of man, and in contrast to the alternative social system which can be put in its place in the process of history.

All of this must be seen in the light of Marx's emphasis in the essays discussed in Chapter 2 on the primacy of economic questions as the chief element to be understood and altered if we are to achieve the answers to the 'theological', 'political' and other question which he treated in those earlier essays.

4

External Critique of Economics and of Economic Life in Terms of Humanist Criteria

And try also, to get rid of personal property. It involves sordid preoccupation, endless industry, continual wrong. . . . So that the recognition of private property has really harmed Individualism. . . . man thought that the important thing was to have, and did not know that the important thing is to be. . . . In fact, property is really a nuisance.

OSCAR WILDE,
The Soul of Man under Socialism

INTRODUCTION

We have seen Marx building his first economic model. He now passes on to: 'a sharp questioning of the economic process as to whether and how it fulfils the real needs of individuals.'[95]

This questioning will of necessity employ criteria which lie outside the scope of economics itself; hence the phrase, the *external critique of economics*. I have used the predicate 'external'. One could as easily speak of Marx's critique as being 'above' (i.e. in human terms *superior to*) or 'below' (i.e. in depth of analysis *more profound than*) the level of discussion of the economists. However we express it, the main point is that Marx evaluates the economic life of his time, and the science which describes that life, in terms of human criteria which, he claims, lie 'above', 'below' or 'outside' the scope of economics itself. Schumpeter somewhat unkindly remarks that it is not easy to raise objections against Marx's critique of economics— 'for, on principle, we may call things what we please.'[96]

This merry quip is, however, a caricature of Marx's methodology. He does not call things what he pleases, rather does he call them what the economists *do not* please to call them. He does so not in the name of some totally vague ideas which he takes up and drops as he sees fit, but rather in the name of a

philosophy of man. This philosophy is, in comparison with
the language of the economists, transcendent and even
'metaphysical', in that it refers to the historical development
of the human species, beyond the narrow, 'eternal' horizons
of the economists. As Bigo puts it: 'from whatever point of
view we confront it, we are thus forced to conclude that
Marxist political economy is permeated throughout by an
affirmation in the metaphysical order.'[97]

We shall accept the predicate 'metaphysical' here simply in
the sense that Marx transcends the scope of the economists;
the more directly philosophical problems of his notion of
transcendence will arise in Chapters 5 and 7.

HUMANIST CRITIQUE OF THE ECONOMISTS

From where does Marx derive his criteria? He has shown us
that the economists, while often correct in their account of the
'first-level facts' of economic life, fail to grasp it as a historical
totality. Thus they regard as autonomous, elements which are
in fact interconnected, and as eternal and immutable, what is
in fact a part of the process of history. It is not surprising,
then, that Marx should propose *historical* criteria for his assessment and critique of economic life. As Kamenka points out:
'Marx expounds no moral "principles", or standards, according
to which political economy is tried and found wanting.'[98]

Rather than assessing economic life and economics as to
their 'goodness' or 'badness' from a static point of view, for
example a timeless conception of human nature, Marx is
concerned to make a historical, developmental critique. What
he will do first of all is grasp the current scene as a totality,
and demonstrate its most fundamental conditions; then he
will locate it as a stage in human history, and show what real
possibilities of transcending it are open to us. If Marx is going
to criticise current reality from a historical perspective, then
his criteria must be those human capacities which in a sense
'underlie' history, in that they are realised in some sense in all
societies, but can be realised more adequately in a new form
of society. Marx builds up, as Marcuse suggests in the quotation
above, what we might call a need-and-capacity frame of
reference; this is based on his anthropology or theory of human
activity, which we shall shortly consider.

Alienation

What Marx tells us about our established social order is that in it man is *alienated*. To summarise the symptoms of human alienation we may say that when he is alienated, man is

(*a*) *impoverished*, as he is less than his true self;

(*b*) *mutilated* by this loss of self;

(*c*) *estranged* from something which is an expression, a creation of his own potentiality, but over which he has lost control;

(*d*) *divided*, because of the contradiction between his present situation and the possible human situation in which he can and should live;

(*e*) *enslaved* because, although liberty is essential to his being and to the expression of that being, he is dominated by his present situation, and by a being outside himself.

The most immediate indication of the alienation of man in contemporary industrial capitalist society is the contrast and conflict between capital, the wealth created by the human species, and the majority of that species, who are reduced to the narrowness of being one-sided, 'abstract' labour: a human factor of production.

Antithesis of Abstract Labour and Abstract Capital

Marx claims that in all societies there has been an antithesis between the active creators of wealth and its passive expropriators.

But the antithesis between *propertylessness* and *property* is still an indeterminate antithesis . . . so long as it is not understood as an antithesis between *labour* and *capital*. (B 152)

This antithesis has come to fruition through the impact of the economic revolution on the feudal economy. In Chapter 2, we have already seen how in the feudal situation, there was the appearance of a human bond between the lord and his serfs; this is what Marx means by the 'political colouring' of feudal society. This social structure was, however, shattered by the economic revolution, in which the economy began to be dominated by the movement of capital, the dynamic, cumulative form of wealth characteristic of the market- and factory-systems. When this happened, it was inevitable:

that the rule of the property owner should appear as the naked rule of private property, of capital, dissociated from all political colouring; that the relation between property owner and worker should be confined to the economic relationship of exploiter and exploited. (B 115)

There is an illuminating parallel between this analysis of the economic revolution, and the analysis of the political revolution which we saw in Chapter 2.[99]

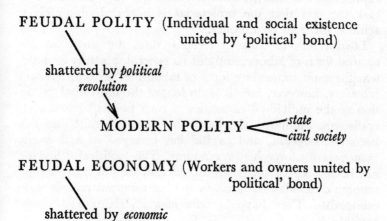

FEUDAL POLITY (Individual and social existence
                united by 'political' bond)

shattered by *political*
     revolution

        MODERN POLITY ← *state*
                        civil society

FEUDAL ECONOMY (Workers and owners united by
                'political' bond)

shattered by *economic*
     revolution

        MODERN ECONOMY ← *capitalists*
                          proletariat

The similarity, however, should not blind us to a crucial difference. In the first model, the terms individual/social and state/civil society apply to each person in the polity. The contradiction involved is between spheres of the life of each person. At the end of Chapter 2, however, we saw how Marx introduced that group who are totally excluded from such political arrangements, namely the proletariat. In Chapter 3, we saw how he analysed the working of the economy, and described some of the conditions of the life of the proletariat. This led him to the second model, in which, as we foresaw in the conclusion to Chapter 2, the terms have a specific socio-economic reference. The contradiction is between two groups of people, not between two spheres of people's lives in the democratic state. The same man can live in the state and civil society; the same man cannot be both a capitalist and a proletarian. The second model now takes over from the first. Here we see the importance of grasping that there was in fact a transition from a 'political' to an 'economic' model. If we assume that the second model is that with which Marx began his career, we shall overlook the search for a real community expressed in the earlier analysis; consequently, we shall overlook the fact that the proletariat is intended ultimately to achieve this real community.[100]

Löwith tells us that 'in [feudal] days the particular and natural form of labour, and not its general, abstract form . . . was the most immediate form of labour.'[101] In the industrial economy, however, labour is no longer the individual expression of the individual capacities of each particular artisan or craftsman. Similarly, the particular *form* of wealth has now become irrelevant, and capital has emerged as a dynamic, homogeneous force in the economy. The 'political colouring' has been swept away, both labour and capital have become economic calculanda, terms in the input-output models of the economists. They have become *abstract* labour and *abstract* capital.

In the context of this argument Marx is able to deal summarily with one of the most complex and bitter controversies of the day. This is the controversy between the established landed interest (immovable property) and the rising industrial capitalist class (movable property).

It is only necessary to read the attacks upon immovable property by representatives of movable property and vice versa, in order to obtain a clear picture of their respective worthlessness. (B 141)

Whatever polemical smoke-screens the landed and industrial interests may put up, they both are forms of exploitation. Moreover, as we saw in Chapter 3,[102] the movement of capital will mean that the former class will soon be as good as subsumed in the latter; the real 'debate', if it be not too polite a term, is between the exploited proletariat and *all* forms of exploitation.

What does this antithesis of abstract capital and abstract labour mean in the concrete life-experience of the worker?

Marx tells us in a neat formulation from the Notes on James Mill, written at the same time as the *EPM*:

his labour can more and more be characterised as wage-labour, until finally it is purely this and it becomes quite accidental and inessential both whether the producer has the immediate enjoyment of a product that he personally needs and also whether the very activity of his labour enables him to enjoy his personality, realise his natural capacities and spiritual aims.[103]

Marx holds this phenomenon of alienated labour to be the basic factor in shaping modern society; it is basic in terms both of fact (as to how the economy functions) and of value (in the sense that it is here that humanity is most debased, and most demands emancipation).

Alienated Labour

Marx tells us how the worker is alienated in the labour-situation. Firstly, he is alienated because the product of his labour:

exists independently, *outside himself*, and alien to him, and . . . it stands opposed to him as an autonomous power. (B 122–3)

The more the worker labours, the more objects he creates. But these objects represent a loss of his powers, because he does not reap the fruits of his labour. In earlier historical periods, man conferred his powers on celestial beings, as in ancient Egypt, India and Mexico (see B 129). But nowadays

the alien being to whom labour and the product of labour belong . . . can only be *man* himself. (B 130)

It is the capitalist who expropriates the product of labour; it is he who is the human alien being on whom the worker confers his own powers and energies. But it would be a mistake to see alienation as merely the *result* of the process of labour:

alienation appears . . . also in the *process* of production, within *productive activity* itself. (B 124)

The labourer

does not fulfil himself in his work but denies himself, has a feeling of misery rather than well-being, does not develop freely his mental and physical energies but is physically exhausted and mentally debased. The worker, therefore, feels himself at home only during his leisure time, whereas at work he feels homeless. It is not his own work but work for someone else. (B 124–5)

Thus the alienated labourer experiences not only *alienation of the thing* (loss of the product of his labour) but also *self-alienation* (loss of self in the process of labour) (see B 126). There is also a third aspect to the matter. We have already seen in Chapter 1 that Marx regards man as a species-being (*Gattungswesen*). This notion will be developed more fully in Chapter 7, but here we must take account of the elements of man's species-being which are relevant to this argument. We have seen that Engels regarded the vast potential for the creation of wealth in the industrial system as the result of the capacities of social rather than isolated man.[104] This point, for Marx, means that man is a species-being in his productive activity. It is the species which acts upon brute nature, the 'inorganic body' of the species (see B 126–7). In the situation of alienated labour, however, each individual is cut off from his fellows, and the natural co-operation which would characterise human work in a human situation is vitiated and frustrated. This *alienation from the species* means that

each man is alienated from others, and that each of the others is likewise alienated from human life. (B 129)

This argument remains vague, until we introduce two other elements, private property and division of labour.

If we examine alienation of the thing more closely, we will realise that it is possible only because some members of society are allowed to appropriate the fruits of the labour of others. The matter, however, is far from simple:

Although private property appears to be the basis and the cause of alienated labour, it is rather a consequence of the latter. . . . At a later stage, however, there is a reciprocal influence. Only in the final stage of the development of private property is its secret revealed, namely, that it is on one hand the *product* of alienated labour, and on the other hand the *means* by which labour is alienated, the realisation of this alienation. (B 131)

Marx holds that it is only because alienated labour is not the free activity of the labourer, directed towards the expression of his own capacities, that it is possible for its product to end up in the hands of another. However, once the system whereby the products of labour are expropriated by non-labourers has been established, these non-labourers acquire a power, they exercise an active role. At this stage, private property intensifies the alienations in labour from which it originally derived, and this is what Marx means by the reciprocal influence of the two.

Let us turn to the division of labour. Division of labour occurs not simply where there is a large group of producers working together, but where each is performing a small and specific part of the work involved in producing the final product. Marx examines the views of the economists on this phenomenon (see B 181–7). He finds that they 'are very confused and self-contradictory about the nature of the division of labour' (B 181).

Some economists see the propensity for division of labour as *innate* to man, others as having been *acquired* through the development of the market and of the factory-system.

The whole of modern political economy is agreed, however, upon the fact that division of labour and abundance of production, division of labour and accumulation of capital, are mutually determining. (B 185)

It is the division of labour, the parcelling of work-activity into narrow and repetitive tasks, which creates the narrowness, the self-alienation, which the worker suffers in the process of labour. Does Marx condemn the division of labour outright, from every point of view? No, for although it is alienating, it is nevertheless a form of species-activity (see B 181). In other words, it shows us that co-operation and social production are essential to the increase of wealth which characterises modern society. Marx would not advocate a return to the small-scale, isolated production characteristic of the poverty and static economy of pre-capitalist societies. The tragedy of the division of labour is that while it is an expression of man's sociality and essential dependence on others, it takes place in a society characterised by the antithesis of labour and capital, and by private property, where 'mutual activity and exchange of activity itself appears as division of labour which makes of man an extremely abstract being, a machine etc., and leads to an abortion of his intellectual and physical faculties'.[105]

These arguments illustrate what Marx means when he tells us that

alienation is apparent not only in the fact that *my* means of life belong to *someone else*, that *my* desires are the unattainable possession of *someone else*, but that everything is *something different* from itself, that my activity is *something else*, and finally (and this is also the case for the capitalist) that *an inhuman power* rules over everything. (B 177–8)

So long as the fundamental conditions of alienation (alienated labour and private property), are in existence, then the fundamental conditions of society are inhuman and anti-social; thus even an expression of man's sociality will appear as 'something else', it will be vitiated by the social context in which it occurs:

thus, the greater and more elaborate appears the power of society inside the private property relationship, the more egoistic, antisocial and alienated from his own essence becomes man.[106]

Marx commends Say (see B 186) for having recognised that the division of labour, while being a development and expression of the capacities of the species, diminishes the individual by condemning him to a narrow and routine life-experience.[107] We are now in a position to list the factors which produce alienation in the life of the labourer:

(*a*) He puts his own energy and intelligence into a product which is then expropriated by another.

(*b*) This means that his labour is not the expression of himself, but a drudgery from which another will benefit.

(*c*) Although modern industrial wealth is in fact a product of men acting together, this species-character of work is vitiated because socially produced wealth is privately appropriated by a few.

(*d*) The division of labour means that each individual is condemned to a narrow and meaningless life-experience.

(*e*) In this system, private property, division of labour and accumulation of capital by a few, all interact to produce alienation of the thing, self-alienation and alienation from the species.

Alienated Labour and the Social Complex

In what precise sense does Marx see alienated labour as the fundamental condition of modern society? We may quickly dismiss any notion that it is essential to Marx's argument to prove either the temporal priority of alienated labour to, say, private property, or that alienated labour is the 'cause' of everything that happens in society. As this and the preceding chapter will have made clear, Marx is far less concerned with explaining a strict linear temporal progression of events than he is with giving an account of social reality as a complex interaction of forces. Thus when he says that alienated labour is fundamental, he means that it is only when man works for another who expropriates his product, and when he loses himself in the process of production, that you can have the complex in which 'private property, acquisitiveness, the separation of labour, capital and land, exchange and competition, value and the devaluation of man, monopoly and competition' (B 121) interact to produce the various aspects of alienation which we have noted. The isolation of alienated labour as fundamental is not a mere detail of Marx's argument. It establishes one of the central points of his philosophy, namely, that all the 'external and apparently accidental conditions' (B 120) and 'alien powers' which affect the worker, while oppressive and apparently insuperable, in fact only hold sway because production and human activity in general are not organised in a human way, where human needs decide the structure of production, exchange and consumption, rather than vice versa. Marx's location of the crux of the social complex in the situation of alienated labour is essential to his conviction of the necessity and possibility of a human reconstruction of the whole pattern of social experience.

The worker is the subjective manifestation of the fact that capital is man wholly lost to himself, just as capital is the objective manifestation of the fact that labour is man wholly lost to himself. (B 137)

Marx's Theory of Human Activity

Having seen Marx's 'reduction' of economic phenomena to the human activity of alienated labour, we must now see how he criticises the society based on alienated labour, and what alternative mode of human activity he proposes as a really possible alternative. It is here that Marx's anthropology, or theory of human activity, comes in: it provides the concepts which subsume and subvert the established social order. The basic concepts in this theory are those of *sense, objectification* and *appropriation*. Marx uses the term 'sense' to refer to

not only the five senses, but also the so-called spiritual senses, the practical senses (desiring, loving etc.). (B 161)

Thus the term as used by Marx stands for something as all-embracing as the terms 'capacities' or 'potentialities' as we might use them; more will be said of this concept shortly.

Granted that we have these 'senses', these capacities for many different expressions of our being, how do we manifest them? Marx is insistent that we can manifest our being, realise ourselves, only through concrete activity in the real world— 'what is life but activity?' (B 126)

We are not ethereal creatures who happen to come down to earth occasionally in order to show what they can do: we only *are* in so far as we express ourselves by action in the objective world:

man is not an abstract being, squatting outside the world. ... Man is affirmed in the objective world. . . . He has real, sensuous objects as the objects of his being . . . he can only express his being in real, sensuous objects. (B 43, 161, 207)

Thus, one moment of all human activity is *objectification*: our activity has the result that we have either created an object ourselves, or transformed an already existing object, so that a part of our selves, a realisation of one of our senses, now stands outside us. Just as Marx's term 'senses' is of unusually wide application, we need not tie the notion of objectification down to the obviously palpable: the scientist with his theories (B 157) or the partners in a human group (B 176) are objectifying human capacities.

But along with the moment of creating objects, there goes necessarily the moment in which man relates to his objectifi-cations, to the being which they have realised for him: this is the moment of *appropriation*:

he sees his own reflection in a world which he has constructed. (B 128)

We may thus characterise all human activity as the objectification of our senses, and our appropriation of that objectification. We have now isolated the anthropological concepts in terms of which Marx will both criticise current modes of activity and propose alternative modes.

Marx tells us what he believes to be characteristic of human activity, as distinct from that of the animals. Of course, animals 'work' in a sense. But while the animal has a kind of consciousness, is conscious *in* its activity, it has not got man's self-consciousness, his consciousness *of* his activity:

the animal is one with its life activity .... But man makes his life activity the object of his will and consciousness. He has a conscious life activity. It is not a determination with which he is completely identified. (B 127)

Moreover, each species of animal is determined both in the material or range of materials on which it acts, and in the type of activity which it exercises upon that material. Man is able to act upon any part of the natural world, applying to each type of material the type of activity proper to it. He can act upon certain materials and produce paper, as does the wasp, and upon certain other types and produce fabrics, as does the spider. Thus man's activity is capable of a freedom not granted to that of any other species (see B 128).

All these points, however, provide us only with a notion of what human activity could ideally be: not that these points do not hold true of work in the present situation, but that the essential freedom, creativity and wholeness of truly human activity appear, as we have already seen, only in an alienated or warped form in the present economic structure. In the contemporary form of society, our objectifications and appropriations are less than adequately human. In terms of his anthropological concepts, Marx can see the answer to one of the chief questions which he has set himself:

what is the significance, in the development of mankind, of this reduction of the greater part of mankind to abstract labour? (B 77)

The significance of this fact, as it emerges in the concrete life experience of each individual worker, is that his senses,

7

and his capacities for expressing them, are restricted. The experience of the worker in the present situation is undifferentiated, in that his work becomes the application of a homogeneous quantum of energy (abstract labour) in a process controlled by abstract capital, the homogeneous alien object which he has created. If Einstein, Mozart and Julius Caesar were all kept at work on a production line, performing all the time the same task, they would be reduced to a dull sameness in that all of them would be deprived of the ability to develop what was unique and specific to them. Our senses are repressed, in that our capacities are allowed to develop only in so far as they do not interfere with the process of production within the division of labour.

But if our way of objectifying ourselves is an undifferentiated drudgery, so also is our way of appropriating objects alienated, less than human. This is because we are dominated by what Marx calls the 'sense of having': under the dominance of necessity, we come to see objects as valuable not for what they are in themselves, for their specific being, but rather, simply as 'things-to-be-possessed':

private property has made us so stupid and one-sided that an object is only *ours* when we have it, when it exists for us as a capital or when it is directly eaten, drunk, worn, inhabited etc., in short, *utilised* in some way. (B 159)

Marx, in other words, is telling us that our way of appropriating objects is also undifferentiated, in that it suppresses the specific nature of each object in a welter of possessiveness.

Money, credit, value: Indeed, Marx argues, we have allowed our possessiveness, our sense of having, to dominate us to such an extent that we have come to value money—which is but a means to the end of possession—as an end in itself.

The complete domination of the alienated thing over man is manifested in money, the complete indifference both with regard to the nature of the material and the specific nature of the private property, and to the personality of the private property owner.[108]

If our appropriation through the sense of having is at one remove, then the cult of money is at two removes, from the human reality which we should be experiencing. In the *Notes on James Mill*, Marx goes into further detail on the way in which private property, the sense of having, and their symbol, money, prevail over human relationships. In the system of exchange which has developed under private property, men are thwarted in their relation both to one another and to objects. As we have seen, the sense of having represses the being of objects; in the *Notes* Marx expresses this by saying that objects are reduced to the status of mere 'equivalence',[109] to being merely instruments to acquire more possessions. Equally, exchange and exchange-value means that the veil of having intervenes in what should be a direct, personal relationship between human beings: the ultimate stage in this is credit, where his possession or lack of money becomes even the *moral judgement* on a man: 'In other words, all the social virtues of the poor man, the whole content of his vital activity, his existence itself represents for the rich man the reimbursing of his capital and its interest.'[110]

The upshot of all this is that the world of things lives an autonomous life, in contempt of human needs and potentialities:

what I *am* and *can do*, is, therefore, not at all determined by my individuality. I *am* ugly, but I can buy the most beautiful woman for myself. . . . I am *stupid*, but since money is the real mind of all things, how should its possessor be stupid? . . . *Money* is the external, universal means and power (not derived from man as man nor from human society as society), to change *representation* into *reality* and *reality* into *mere representations*. (B 191, 193)

Truly human activity: Marx completes his critique by suggesting the conditions for truly human activity. He holds that 'sense which is subservient to crude needs has only a restricted meaning' (B 161–2) and proposes 'the complete emancipation of all the human qualities and senses' (B 160).

Each of the aspects of our being will be objectified in the way suited to it, rather than being subsumed under abstract labour through necessity. Equally, man will have developed the capacity to appropriate the world of objects in the specific way suited to the kind of object in question:

the most beautiful music has no meaning for the non-musical ear, is not an object for it, because my object can only be the confirmation of one of my own faculties. It can only be so for me in so far as my faculty exists as a subjective capacity, because the meaning of an object for me extends only as far as the sense extends (only makes sense for an appropriate sense). (B 161)

When man has achieved truly human activity, he will:

appropriate his manifold being in an all-inclusive way, and thus as a whole man. All his human relations to the world—seeing, hearing, smelling, tasting, touching, thinking, observing, feeling, desiring, loving—in short, all the organs of his individuality . . . are in their objective action (their action in relation to the object) the appropriation of this object, the appropriation of human reality. (B 159)

The reader should not be startled by the unsurprising nature of this list of 'senses'. Marx is not proposing for the new society some hitherto quite unknown type of human activity, some as yet unexplored dimension of human reality. What he *is* saying is that once we are no longer dominated in our objectifications by the labour pattern, and in our appropriation by the sense of having, we shall be able to develop and express in their own right all these capacities, which hitherto have been allowed only in so far as they contribute to, or at least do not hinder, the overcoming of necessity.

Truly social activity: We have already seen that alienation from the species is an aspect of the situation in which we are alienated from ourselves and from the products of our activity. We are alienated from our fellow-men in our objectification, in the sense that this should be a really, humanly, social activity rather than a mechanically imposed collective drudgery. We are alienated from them in our appropriation in so far as the sense of having, just like the Rights of Man,[111] posits each man's fulfilment as inimical to that of others. The *Notes on James Mill* bring out clearly the point that appropriation-through-having is destructive not only of our relationship to objects, but also of that to our fellows:

man—and this is the basic presupposition of private property— only produces in order to have . . .; not only does production have this utilitarian aim; it also has a selfish aim; man produces only his own exclusive possession.[112]

Alienation from the species occurs in the concrete life

experience of the alienated worker, and not in some mysterious region elevated above that experience; it will likewise be overcome in our concrete life-experience, and not in some abstract sphere, like Hegel's state removed from civil society, over and above that experience. It would thus be a mistake to look for the sense in which man is now 'at one' with his fellows *as well as* having abolished self-alienation and alienation of his products. The *Notes on James Mill* bring out at somewhat greater length the positive alternative to alienation from the species which Marx envisages in the *EPM*:

In your enjoyment or use of my product I would have had the direct enjoyment of realising that I had both satisfied a human need by my work and also objectified the human essence and therefore fashioned for another human being the object that met his need. ... I would have been for you the mediator between you and the species and thus been acknowledged and felt by you as a completion of your own essence and a necessary part of yourself and thus realised that I am confirmed both in your thought and in your love. ... In my expression of my life I would have fashioned your expression of your life, and thus in my own activity have realised my own essence, my human, my communal essence.[113]

In one and the same set of objectifications and appropriations I will realise myself, the specific nature of objects and my fellow-man, instead of losing myself, suppressing the being of objects and competing with my fellows.

The senses and minds of other men have become my *own* appropriation. Thus besides ... direct organs, *social* organs are constituted, in the form of society; for example, activity in direct association with others has become an organ for the manifestation of life and a mode of appropriation of *human* life. (B 160)

Marx's ideal of a form of really human, really social activity and experience, where relationships of men with others and with humanised objects will not be vitiated by the division of labour, by competition, having and money, may be summarised to conclude this section:

Let us assume *man* to be *man*, and his relation to the world to be a human one. Then love can only be exchanged for love, trust for trust, etc. If you wish to enjoy art you must be an artistically cultivated person; if you wish to influence other people you must be a person who really has a stimulating and encouraging effect upon others. Every one of your relations to man and to nature must be a *specific expression*, corresponding to the object of your will, of your *real individual* life. If you love without evoking love in return, i.e. if you are not able, by the *manifestation* of yourself as a loving person, to make yourself a *beloved person*, then your love is impotent and a misfortune. (B 194)

THE REJECTION OF CRUDE COMMUNISM

We have now traced some of the main features of the future society which Marx envisages. This is his ideal of the developed communist society, of which we shall see more in Chapter 7. He examines some other proposed solutions to the problem of private property, and rejects them as taking a one-sided or partial view, or both, of that problem. The only solution which goes to the root of the matter is communism, which is

the positive expression of the abolition of private property, and in the first place [the expression] of universal private property. (B 152)

Communism in this form, however, is merely 'crude'. Its answer to the situation where some own things to the exclusion of others is that all should own things to the exclusion of none:

the relation of private property remains the relation of the community to the world of things. (B 153)

In other words, crude communism universalises, but does not abolish, the sense of having. This form of communism would simply negate the dimensions of human experience which cannot be appropriated by 'immediate physical possession [which] seems to it the unique goal of life and existence.' (B 153)

It also envisages the universal prostitution of women rather than a relationship based on genuine human need for the other person:

The first positive annulment of private property, crude communism, is, therefore, only a *phenomenal form* of the infamy of private property representing itself as positive community. (B 155)

We may summarise both Marx's criticism of crude communism, and the form of developed communism which he

envisages, by saying that he wants to replace the undifferentiated sense of *having* by the sense of *being*; man will be
concerned to express his being in objects and relationships,
and to respond to that being which he has objectified.

CAN LABOUR BE HUMANISED?

We have seen that one of the conditions for real human
community is the elimination of economic necessity. The
question which we now face is: can labour, which even at its
best is human activity in the economic pattern, dominated by
necessity, be a really human activity? I have here employed
a systematic division into the two separate discussions of
alienated labour and of the really *human* types of activity, in
order to pose clearly this question, which is central to Marx's
thought, and which he does not answer conclusively at least
in the *EPM*. Marx is extremely vague about the alternative
he envisages as the cure to the alienated labour-situation. We
may derive a clue from an earlier discussion of the land
question, where he advocates what he calls a form of association.
When the land is worked in this way, we find that:

association . . . has the advantage from an economic point of view
of large-scale ownership, while at the same time it realises . . .
equality. . . . The land ceases to be an object of sordid speculation,
and through the freedom of work and enjoyment becomes once
more man's real personal property. (B 116)

In the *EPM*, Marx does not propose specific answers to the
alienations of the labour-situation. He *may* envisage some form
of co-operative industry in which there will no longer be a
division of owners and workers. He may envisage that the
products of labour will be distributed through some social
mechanism other than the present one of private property. If
such a system were implemented, there might well be reductions
in alienation of the thing, self-alienation in the process of
labour, and alienation from the species. But if we compare
such a set of arrangements with the truly human types of
activity which Marx proposes for the developed communist
society, we will find it less than ideal. *Any* labour-situation will
be one where man works in the economic pattern, under the
dominance of necessity, where he will not develop each of his

senses in their own right, as Marx envisages his doing in the ideal society.

This raises the point about the division of labour. Marx himself has said that although the division of labour takes place in an alienating labour-situation, it is still an expression of 'human activity as species-activity' (B 181).

Marx quite clearly does not propose that we should regress to the feudal form of production, where individual artisans worked in isolation; such a form of production could never achieve the wealth created in industrial society. Some form of division of labour is, in other words, essential to any developed form of labour. Roger Garaudy argues that Marx is opposed only to the division of labour *in a class society* dominated by private property in the means of production: 'A solidarity is affirmed by the division of labour, which solidarity is negated by private property.'[114]

Thus, Garaudy claims, Marx would accept that man in communist society could perform a specialised function, but not be alienated, because he would no longer see his labour as directed to the fulfilment of another than himself, and would not see another expropriating the product of that labour.[115]

We need not deny that it is possible to humanise the labour-situation by introducing various alternatives to the separation of owners and workers, and to the distribution of goods through private property. Such alternatives may well be feasible, although Marx does not elaborate them in the *EPM*. It is made quite clear in the *EPM*, however, that on the criteria which Marx proposes for truly human and truly social activity, man cannot truly fulfil himself in any activities characterised by necessity, the sense of having and the division of labour.

This discontinuity between his criteria for truly human activity and his analysis of the labour-situation is not merely a feature of Marx's extreme youth. Georges Friedmann conducts an examination of Marx's ideas about these problems, in which he bases his argument solely on Marx's last work, *Das Kapital*. He says that Marx at one point in his analysis seems to believe that a fully human labour-activity is possible; he wants

to replace the detail worker of today, crippled by life-long repetition of one and the same trivial occupation, . . . by the fully developed

individual . . . to whom the different social functions he performs
are but so many modes of giving free scope to his own natural and
acquired powers.[116]

Friedmann argues, however,[117] that Marx changes his mind
in Volume III of the work, and realises that this ideal can be
achieved only outside the pattern of economic activity. 'The
work that millions of men and women do every day for a
living neither enriches their lives nor acts as a balancing
factor. . . . It is the time spent away from work, as Marx . . .
saw, that should constitute the "true realm of freedom" for
mankind.'[118] Marx describes this realm of freedom in the
third volume of *Kapital*:

beyond [the realm of necessity] begins that development of human
potentiality for its own sake, the true realm of freedom, which
however can only flourish upon that realm as its basis. The
shortening of the working day is its fundamental pre-requisite.[119]

In an early section of the *EPM*, Marx quotes an argument
from Wilhelm Schulz to the effect that

a nation which aims to develop its culture more freely can no
longer remain the slave of its material needs. . . . It needs above all
leisure *time* in which to produce and enjoy culture. . . . It has been
calculated that in France, at the present level of production, an
average of five hours' work daily would suffice to meet all the
material needs of society. . . . In spite of the saving of time through
the improvement in machinery the duration of slave labour in
factories has increased for a large number of people. (B 79)[120]

Thus, in the *EPM*, Marx is at least aware of the potential
of machinery to liberate man from the pattern imposed by
necessity. This brings us to an interesting observation. On the
one hand we have Friedmann, basing his analysis on *Das
Kapital*, who says that Marx comes *late in his career* to the
conclusion that man must eventually abolish necessity and
labour altogether. On the other hand we have Herbert
Marcuse, who warns us that 'we have dwelt rather extensively
upon Marx's early writings because they emphasise tendencies
that have been attenuated in the post-Marxian development
of his critique of society . . . [such as] *the subordination of [other]
factors to the idea of the free realisation of the individual*. Under all
aspects, however, Marx's early writings are mere preliminary

stages to his mature theory, stages that should not be over-emphasised.'[121]

Let us be precise about what we have established. All we have seen is that, at least in regard to the 'realm of human freedom', the tension which Friedmann notes in Marx's latest works, and Marcuse notes in the earlier works,[122] between labour and truly human activity, would appear to be an enduring element in Marx's thought throughout his career. We have not resolved this tension, because if Marx ever proposed a solution to it, he certainly did not do so in the *Essays and EPM*. Bigo describes a phase in Marx's thinking, between the *EPM* and *Das Kapital*, in which he does appear to accept that there can be a 'half-way stage' where the antithesis of labour and capital will have been abolished, and where a form of social production and social distribution will humanise labour to some extent.[123] Marx does not, however, propose any such explicit half-way stage in the *EPM*; consequently, our analysis can show merely that there is an unresolved tension in those early writings, which tension would appear to persist right up to Marx's very latest period. Robert Tucker gives a very brief summary of Marx's theory of activity as we have seen it. He gives evidence of Marx's constant opposition, throughout his later works, to the division of labour, and discusses the notion of a realm of true human freedom as this appears in *Das Kapital*. Tucker's analysis of these topics in the post-*EPM* writings reflects what would appear to be the tension within Marx's own mind between the attempt to humanise labour and the need to abolish it altogether.[124]

THE MOVEMENT OF ECONOMIC THOUGHT

Marx analyses the movement of economic thought, as a reflection of the historical movement from feudal to industrial society. The first schools he notes are the Mercantilists and their off-shoot, the Bullionists.[125] These two schools regarded precious metals as being wealth *in themselves*, and thus they located wealth in an object totally outside man (see B 147). Avineri tells us that Marx considers fetishism to be the phenomenon whereby 'an expression of human creativity appears to be a natural object.'[126] It is in this sense that Marx holds that the Mercantilists are, as Adams puts it, 'the catholics, the fetish-worshippers of political economy, . . . who worshipped private property in its material, symbolic, non-human form in the precious metals.'[127]

In the late eighteenth century, these were succeeded by the French Physiocrats. These latter grasped one of the most important new features of the industrial world, namely that wealth had become a dynamic, self-propagating force. But they located wealth in the land, and their insight into the emergence of dynamic industrial wealth is marred by the fact that

they reject the industrial system and accept the feudal system by declaring that agriculture is the sole industry. (B 150)

Finally, the Classical school come along. They have the insight into the dynamic character of industrial wealth, and moreover see that it is in essence *capital*, in other words wealth which is free from all natural determinations, which can take on any natural form and is confined to none. Also, they grasp the fact that man himself is the creator of this wealth. Thus

Adam Smith [is] the Luther of political economy . . . just as [Luther] annulled external religiosity while making religiosity the inner essence of man . . . ; so wealth external to man and independent of him is annulled. (B 147)

But, we may well ask, does not Marx's section on money suggest that modern man is no more advanced than the Mercantilists? Does not Marx say that in the modern economy we regard money, a being outside ourselves, as an end in itself; do not we even endow it with a life of its own? How then can we say that there has been any progress since the time of the 'catholics and fetish-worshippers'? The answer points to the inherent contradiction in the thought of the modern political economists. With one part of their minds they see that man himself is the source, and should be the master, of wealth; with the other, however, they conveniently overlook the debasement of man, and the fact that the modern industrial system reduces him to a position where he is in fact still a fetish-worshipper, dominated by the cults of possession and of money. In one element of its *thought* economics has progressed since the time of the Mercantilists; but economic life in essence has not changed, because the welfare of man is ignored both by the industrial system and by its reflection-in-thought, political economy.

Political economy at one and the same time says that man, the labourer, is the creator of the modern industrial economy, and accepts that the economy should destroy the labourer. It is not accidental to political economy to disregard all considerations of human welfare; it is of its very essence:

Ricardo lets political economy speak its own language; he is not to blame if this language is not that of morals. (B 173)

Thus we see the point of describing Marx's critique of economics and of economic life as one conducted in terms which are external to economics. 'Political economy *ends* thus precisely at the point where Marx's critique *begins*.'[128]

We can understand Marx's argument in the light of his theory of human activity, as outlined earlier. In a situation where man is dominated by the pattern imposed by necessity, both his life and his consciousness will be divided. All the manifestations of his true humanity will be repressed, and economic thought will predominate to the exclusion of those branches of thought, such as morality, which refer to man's welfare. Thus economics will have no reference to morality, and morality will be powerless in the face of economics (see B 173).

5

Marx Criticises Hegel's General Philosophy

It was as though the tide came up every century,
generation after generation, to submerge again the
islands that the previous age had brought to light;
and so, every time they had to be charted anew,
at an immense expenditure of toil and talent.

PAUL HAZARD,
European Thought in the Eighteenth Century

INTRODUCTION

I have laid some stress on Marx's commitment to two complementary tasks at one and the same time. He is attempting to
discover what are the facts of the world in which he lives, and
at the same time he is attempting to find criteria for the correct
critical attitude. This latter will have two aspects. Firstly, it
will need to be a correct orientation *to* the facts, one which
will not blind our eyes to the real problems of the real world.
Secondly it will need to proceed correctly *from* our knowledge
of those facts and problems; it will have to issue in a practice
that will change the world in accordance with the correct
ideas. This latter point was implicit in the criticisms of the
practical and theoretical parties in Chapter 2, and will be
developed in Chapter 6.

Although as I have said the two searches are simultaneous
and complementary, they do not receive equal emphasis at all
times. Thus we may say that in the passages examined in
Chapter 2 to 4, Marx has been concerned mainly with finding
out the facts, the facts both of the actual situation and of the
possible alternative world. We now come to the last of the
writings contained in the *EPM*, which is Marx's final systematic
and explicit critique of Hegel's philosophy. In this chapter,
as we shall see, we are concerned with Marx's search for a
correct critical stance, in the two aspects outlined above,
rather than with discussion of facts. Having given his own

account of political and economic life, Marx now conducts a systematic appraisal of Hegel's critical stance, in which his concern is primarily to discover the essential elements of an acceptable alternative stance.

CRITIQUE OF HEGEL'S DIALECTIC AND GENERAL PHILOSOPHY[129]

Marx begins, characteristically enough, with an attack. The object of his scorn is the 'Critical School', exemplified by Bruno Bauer and *Die Freien*, whom Marx had in more than a geographical sense left behind him in Berlin. These critics have set themselves up in a self-subsistent ideal universe, regard themselves as the sole repositories of philosophical truth, and regard the real world, and its inhabitants, the 'masses' with undisguised contempt. They sit

enthroned in sublime solitude, content to utter occasionally from [their] sarcastic lips the laughter of the Olympian gods. (B 197)

They consider that they have only one task—to analyse the world philosophically. This done, they sit content in their own critical universe, leaving the real world and its mortal inhabitants to go their own foolish way.

Only one post-Hegelian philosopher has grappled with

the partly formal, but in fact *essential* question—how do we now stand with regard to the Hegelian dialectic? (B 195)

This is Feuerbach. Only he has shown that Hegelian philosophy is just as divorced from the real world as is religious consciousness. He has called for its replacement by a genuine science of man, an anthropology based on empirical discovery of the relations between real men in the real world. He has opposed this science to the Hegelian 'negation of the negation', which is in essence merely the attempt to resolve in thought problems which we have fundamentally misconstrued by posing them as theoretical rather than practical problems. Marx now proceeds to settle his own account with the Hegelian system.

This system he regards as an idealist monism. In other words, it posits one sole ultimate reality, and that ultimate reality is thought in its most developed form, or Absolute

Spirit. The main theme of Marx's critique is that this idealist monism leads Hegel to an incorrect conception of man, of the objective world, and finally of the relations between these two.

Let us deal firstly with the objective world in which we live. In Hegel's system, the first guise under which this world appears is the category of Nature, or spirit-in-its-otherness. It is spirit which has externalised itself. Thus the world is spirit estranged from itself. Marx says that for Hegel

Nature is external to [abstract thought], loss of itself, and is only conceived as something external, as abstract thought, but alienated abstract thought. (B 200)

Thus his first criticism of Hegel is that idealist monism cannot allow any real status to the objective world. If thought is the ultimate reality, then the world of objects must be something inferior, a transient phenomenon of spirit-in-its-otherness. Mende presents Marx as arguing that in Hegel, 'objective reality is presented not in its materiality, that is, in its independence *vis-à-vis* consciousness, but rather as the absolute idea, as world-spirit.'[130]

How does Hegel conceive man? Marx says that he sees man as being essentially consciousness, and this consciousness as a moment in the life of spirit.

The way in which consciousness is, and in which something is for it, is *knowing*. Knowing is its only act. (B 209)

Now Marx has said that Hegel sees:

(*a*) Man as *consciousness*,

(*b*) the objective world as a mere phenomenon of *spirit*, and

(*c*) man's relation to this world as one of *knowing*.

In opposition to these conceptions, Marx believes that:

(*a*) man is an *objective being*,

(*b*) the objective world is the real and necessary realm in which man fulfils himself, and that

(*c*) man's relation to the world is one of *activity* rather than of knowing.

The meaning of these propositions will emerge more clearly as we see Marx's discussion of Hegel.

Marx claims that Hegel defines man as consciousness. Man confronts the world, and finds it alien to him, because objectivity has the appearance of having a hard shell which thought cannot penetrate. However, as we pass from this level of mere understanding to that of reason, we come to see that the objective world is merely composed of particular instantiations of universal forms of thought (colour, size, quality and so forth). Now if spirit is the highest form of thought, we find that both man and the world, properly understood, are moments in the life of spirit; man as consciousness, the world as spirit-in-its-otherness, as thought estranged from itself. Once man reaches this point of reflection, it is impossible that he should continue to feel strange in the world, and thus he has overcome his alienation in thought. Here we see how, Marx alleges, Hegel conceives the three important moments—man, the world and the relation of the two—as essentially matters of thought.

Let us see firstly Marx's rejection of the definition of man as consciousness. Man, Marx claims, is an objective being:

the fact that man is an embodied, living, real, sentient, objective being with natural powers, means that he has real sensuous objects as the objects of his being, or that he can only express his being in real, sensuous objects. (B 209)

This argument follows directly from the schema of activity drawn up in Chapter 4. In our discussion of activity (which of course, Marx sees as the whole of man's life) we saw that every mode of activity requires an objectification.

Let us now turn to Hegel's conception of the objective world. Here we find that:

it is not the fact that the human being objectifies himself inhumanly, in opposition to himself, but that he objectifies himself in opposition to abstract thought, which constitutes alienation as it exists and as it has to be transcended. . . . It is not the determinate character of the object but its objective character which is the scandal for self-consciousness. (B 201 and 209)

Marx argues that Hegel's positing of spirit as sole ultimate reality means that the objective world, that which is not spirit, is conceived not in its own right but in its relation to spirit. This relation is necessarily one of inferiority; the world is merely the 'otherness' of spirit. This, he claims, leads Hegel into a serious error. Hegel concludes that man is alienated in the present objective world *because it is an objective world*. He fails to see that it is merely the present form of the objective world, the 'determinate character' of the world, which is alienating. Avineri puts this point well by saying that for Marx 'alienation and objectification, which overlap phenomenologically in present society, will be radically distinguished in the future, when alienation will disappear.'[131]

Marx argues that Hegel's idealism is itself 'unhappy' with its inability to give any real status to the objective world. It is conscious of its own circularity. This circularity emerges in the attempt to grasp the nature of the thing, namely that which by definition is set over against thought. All that the Hegelian system can come up with is the *thought* of the thing ('thinghood') which is of course a self-contradictory result. The circularity of this attempt leads idealism, which cannot grasp the real world on its own rational premises, to leap into some mystical 'intuition' of the world as Nature.

The mystical feeling which drives the philosopher from abstract thinking to intuition is ennui, the longing for a content. (B 216)

Thus far, Marx has argued two of his three charges against the Hegelian conception of the world. He has accused it of seeing man as consciousness rather than as an objective being, and of seeing the world as essentially, rather than merely in its present form, inimical to man's fulfilment. He also claims that the definition of man as consciousness must lead to a misconception of his relation to the world, because

the way in which consciousness is, and in which something is for it, is *knowing*. Knowing is its only act. (B 209)

Thus, man's alienation in the world is essentially an alienation of consciousness, an alienation in and of the mind. This leads Hegel to say that the proper response to an alien objective situation is not to change it but to know it. We do not act upon the world so as to improve it; we simply pass in thought from the initial position of understanding to the higher level of reason. Thus our overcoming of the situation is merely a 'supersession in thought'.

This supersession in thought, which leaves its object in existence in the real world, believes itself to have really overcome it. (B 212)

8

When Marx turns from this attack on the three misconceptions involved in Hegel's system to the unacceptable result to which these misconceptions lead, we are confronted with a paradox. In the first place, we have seen that Hegel regards objectivity as being what we may call ontologically inferior to spirit, to ultimate reality. In more popular terms, we may say that Hegel's system involves a 'downgrading' of the real world in favour of pure thought. This explains why he conceives man's overcoming of alienation as a process of thought rather than of action. But a paradox arises when we look more closely at this supersession 'in which denial and preservation, denial and affirmation, are linked together' (B 211).

The puzzle is that the positing of objectivity as ontologically inferior issues in a defence and affirmation of the particular objective arrangements of the world as we find it—what Marx calls 'the existing empirical world' (B 201). If man is told that the objective world, no matter what its particular historical form, is essentially inimical to his fulfilment, and can be overcome only by seeing it as a phenomenon of spirit, by superseding it in thought, then he will eventually argue himself into a position where he confers an undue importance on the world in its given form, precisely because he has learnt to see it as an affirmation of ultimate reality.

Since the object has become for [him] a 'moment' of thought, it is regarded in its real existence as a confirmation of thought, of consciousness, of abstraction. (B 212)

It is thus that Marx claims that

there can no longer be any question about Hegel's compromise with religion, the state, etc., for this falsehood is the falsehood of his whole argument. (B 210)

When Hegel has examined all the objective constituents of man's social universe, and seen them only as incomplete and partial, he tells us that by reflecting on these objective constituents we can come to see them not in their immediate, alien form, but as moments in the life of spirit. This attitude is clearly that which 'downgrades' the objective world. But when this has all happened, we still find that 'in actuality private right, morality, the family, civil society, the state etc. remain' (B 211).

Hegel's man is the type who starts off by crying over spilt milk (the Unhappy Consciousness confronted by the objective world). Then he begins to 'philosophise' about it, and dries his eyes, because he has come to know the situation as it really is. Marx's man will immediately point out that this is all very well, but the milk is still on the floor. He will reach for the mop and do something about it. Hegel's man, however, still retains one potent defence. He will regard the antics of his friend with an amused contempt, and point out to him how silly it is to get one's knees dirty trying to clean the floor, when all the situation demands is a little high-level reflection. Marx's man cannot be content simply to make known his disagreement with the Hegelian notion of philosophical fulfilment; he has yet to show that this is in fact not a fulfilment at all, but merely an illusion. This indicates an aspect of man as objective being which Marx does not draw out at length in this essay. It is not enough for Marx to say that man *can* fulfil himself in the objective world; he must show that he has no alternative but to do so. Marx's critique of Hegel must be total, or it becomes ineffective. If he allows even one chink through which fulfilment-in-thought may enter, he then faces the problem of deciding how far we act upon the world, and how far, by contrast, we accept it as it is. Marx's man cannot allow himself even to think about thinking about the spilt milk, for if he does so he has 'compromised' with the world as it is, he has affirmed rather than denied the situation. Thus in the terms of Marx's argument, the conflict comes down to an irreconcilable divergence between one system which (*a*) denies the reality of the world on the ontological level, and (*b*) paradoxically, affirms the reality of the present conditions of that world, and a system which (*a*) affirms the reality of the objective world on the ontological level and (*b*) denies the reality of the present historical world as we find it.

We have now isolated one of the elements of a critical stance which Marx would regard as superior to Hegel's. This is, that it must not deny the ultimate reality of the world in which men live and, in doing so, project him into an illusory universe of pure thought. We may well ask whether this condition, while necessary, is sufficient for a correct stance. Here a problem arises for Marx. There exists a well-established philosophical school, that represented pre-eminently by the French materialists, which admirably fulfils this condition. In fact, they do so with such enthusiasm that they come to doubt the reality of anything *but* the material world. Is this the stance which Marx proposes? He hastens to make it clear that this is quite as unacceptable as Hegel's position. We shall see in Chapter 6 precisely why he does so, but may anticipate to the extent of saying that the materialist alternative to Hegel, by failing to allow any role to human consciousness, makes man as much a prisoner of matter, in Marx's opinion, as Hegel makes him a prisoner of spirit. Marx only hints at the simultaneous rejection of these two monisms by saying that his own position, which he calls:

consistent naturalism or humanism is distinguished from both idealism and materialism, and at the same time constitutes their unifying truth. (B 206)

We should not close this exposition without referring to the merits which Marx sees in Hegel's system. One of these is that

Hegel grasps the self-creation of man as a process, objectification as loss of the object, as alienation and transcendence of this alienation. (B 202)

In other words, Hegel's system is the first to give a real account of man as a historical being, one who makes his own world. Equally, it describes the imperfections of the world as it at present exists. Indeed, Marx allows,

all the elements of criticism are contained in it, and are often presented and worked out in a manner which goes far beyond Hegel's own point of view. (B 202)

It is this last observation that gives us the clue to the real defect which Marx alleges. Because of Hegel's own point of view, all the elements of his account are misconceived. He sees the world as a product of man, but of cognitive, not active, man. He sees many of the imperfections of the present objective world, but again, because of his point of view, concludes that the world is essentially—rather than in its present form—inadequate to man's fulfilment. In spite of this defect in Hegel's thinking, Marx recognises that he says much in certain sections of his account, which, given an alternative point of view such as that which Marx himself proposes, adds immensely to our knowledge of the facts of our present situation. Indeed, in many such discussions, Hegel comes so close to accepting the reality of the world that he actually goes far beyond his own fundamental point of view.

But, Marx claims, he ultimately fails to grasp the full facts of man's situation. For example, his ability to ignore the real world and to 'interpret' it in terms of his own philosophical categories means that although he regards labour as one of the most important features of man's life, he does not see the distinction between the potentialities of human labour and its present alienating form.

> Hegel's standpoint is that of modern political economy. He conceives labour as the essence, the self-confirming essence, of man; he observes only the positive side of labour, not its negative side. (B 203)

If Hegel had affirmed that man could fulfil himself in the world, he would have seen the distinction between the alienating conditions of the present and a possible alternative world in which alienation would be abolished. As it is, labour figures only as an abstract philosophical category in his idealist system.

MARX'S AND HEGEL'S NOTIONS OF PHILOSOPHY

Marx's criticisms of Hegel's philosophical conceptions of man, the world and their relation are underpinned by his radical contesting of Hegel's notion of the very nature and purpose of philosophy itself. We may conclude this exposition of Marx's criticism by considering this radical contesting. As we have seen, Marx does not deny that Hegel is well aware of many of the defects of the given world. Where he fundamentally disagrees with Hegel is on the question of how we are to 'transcend', to go beyond, these defects. The issue may be briefly stated as one between transcendence-in-thought and historical transcendence.

According to Marx, Hegel sees the function of philosophy in the following way. Faced by a hostile, alien and unintelligible world, the philosopher reflects to the point where he sees that world as merely one accidental form in which the 'basic' abstractions—such as 'consciousness', 'spirit', 'nature', 'objectivity' and so forth—have been realised or made concrete. In this sense, Hegelian philosophy dissolves the real, empirical world, and reduces it to empty abstractions. At this point, the Hegelian philosopher claims to have 'transcended' or overcome the given social world, in the sense that he has gone beyond it to the abstractions of which it is a mere outward appearance. Hegelian philosophy would claim to liberate us from the narrowness and imperfections of our situation, whatever that situation may be, by showing us the fundamental structure which underlies it: when we, who are essentially consciousness-in-the-world, grasp that this fundamental process is that of spirit, the highest form of consciousness, then we are once more at home, we have transcended the strangeness of our world.

But Marx claims that Hegelian philosophy has in this way not overcome, but simply abstracted from, the real world: 'For its real mode of existence is *abstraction*' (B 200). When those living in nineteenth-century capitalist society grasp the fundamental structure underlying their world, they have grasped the same structure as they would have grasped had they lived in feudal or Greek society. To find relief or escape from the world's limitations in the pseudo-infinity of idealist abstractions is not, according to Marx, an overcoming of, but rather a flight from, our real problems. The terms of Hegelian philosophy

are, therefore, general, abstract *forms of abstraction* which refer to any content and are thus neutral towards, and valid for, any content; forms of thought, logical forms which are detached from *real* spirit and *real* nature. (B 215)

When Marx, in the same context, tells us that '*logic* is the *money* of the mind, the speculative thought-value of man and of nature, their essence indifferent to any real determinate character and thus unreal' (B 200) he does not choose his comparison lightly. As we saw in Chapter 4, money is the supreme expression of the fact that the individual, specific characteristics of both men and objects have become submerged in an undifferentiated morass of *having*. Now Marx is telling us that the philosophical abstractions, the logical thought-forms of Hegelian idealism are incapable of grappling with the intractability and specificity of the real, concrete and complex world in which we find ourselves. It is not only the Hegelian forms of thought which are 'indifferent' to the content of our given world: we ourselves are taught to become indifferent to the 'content' of our particular world, to our social reality. This is what a transcendence-in-thought amounts to: we learn to forget, rather than actively to humanise, our imperfect situation.

If transcendence-in-thought is a flight from empirical reality in favour of idealist abstractions, Marx argues that there is another possibility: a *historical* transcendence, or an active rejection and transformation of empirical reality in the direction of a new social reality. This is the force of Marx's criticism of the Theoretical Party:[132]

its principal defect may be summarised as follows: it believed that it could realise philosophy without abolishing it. (B 51)

In other words, the content of a valid philosophical critique must not be abstractions which have neither much nor little to do with any and all forms of society: it must be a project capable of complete translation into a new form of society:

The philosophers have only *interpreted* the world in different ways; the point is to change it.[133]

For Marx, a valid transcendence of our given world is not a transcendence *above* that world to the realms of idealist speculation: it is not a leap out of history which leaves behind both the defects and the challenges of the world. Authentic transcendence is a transcendence *beyond* the given situation, within the dimensions of human history, to a new and more adequately human society.

Marx develops his charge that Hegelian idealism is both unable and unwilling to grapple with the real empirical world. Because it posits thought as the sole ultimate reality, everything that stands over against thought is reduced to mute indifference: the specific characters of different societies, and of the elements of any given social complex, are reduced to being merely 'objectifications of spirit'. Just as Bauer's idealist speculative group, *Die Freien*, 'has reduced all dogmatic antitheses to the single dogmatic antithesis between its own cleverness and the stupidity of the world' (B 196) so idealist philosophy sees only the opposition in thought itself between abstract thought and sensible reality or real sensuous existence. All other contradictions and movements are merely the *appearance*, the *cloak*, the *exoteric* form of these two opposites which are alone important and which constitute the *significance* of the other, profane contradictions. (B 201)

Marx is here repeating, in a more technical manner, the charge which he made in his *Critique of Hegel's Philosophy of the State* (1843), that Hegel tries to deduce the complexities of the real world from a 'single, abstract principle'.[134] He also puts in compressed technical language a point that we have seen him make earlier in this present chapter. He has argued that the alleged 'supersession' of the given social world by Hegelian philosophy in fact leaves private right, morality and so forth in existence. Hegelian critique would teach us to despise the real world and the real source of our problems and to live in the realms of philosophy where we overcome religion by the *philosophy of religion*, politics by the *philosophy of politics*, and nature in the *philosophy of nature*. But in fact all that this philosophical transcendence has 'overcome' is the *thought* of religion, politics and nature: the real objects are no whit transformed by our inner intellectual transformations. Hegelian transcendence-in-thought is thus 'the philosophical dissolution and restoration of the existing empirical world'. (B 200)

Thus Hegel's notion of the function of philosophy, as Marx sees it, is the following: philosophy dissolves a given social world into its constitutive abstractions, and by leading us to an intellectual grasp of these abstractions and of the relation of ourselves and our world to them, transcends the imperfections of the world by reflection. Marx rejects this notion of philosophy, and, instead, takes as his point of departure an analysis of the real, empirical world in its complexity, specificity and autonomy *vis-à-vis* consciousness; from this he proceeds, through revolutionary action within the dimensions of terrestrial history, to the implementation of a project whose contents are exhausted by its application in reality.

IS MARX'S ACCOUNT OF HEGEL FAIR?

Let us briefly review the different aspects of man's experience dealt with in the Hegelian system. We find an account of the development of man's consciousness, from its first primitive grappling with the world at the level of understanding, through the phase of dialectic, to the higher level of reason, the pinnacle of philosophical reflection (*The Phenomenology of Mind*).[135] We find similarly an analysis of the nature and forms of thought as they are related and as they develop to embrace the complexity of being (*The Logic*).[136] We also find an account of the various dimensions of man's experience in society, from his immediate, primitive subjectivity to the level of concrete, realised community (*The Philosophy of Right*).[137] As man is a historical being we have also an account of all the phases of human history, treated from the point of view of their significance for man in the present historical situation of which they are the genesis (*The Philosophy of History*).[138] These are the main elements of a system which, as we already suggested, sets out to give an exhaustive account of what it means to be human.

Marx sets out, as we have also seen, to answer a different question. From Marx's starting point, Hegel's system naturally can be summarised as an insidious attempt to reconcile man to his present situation, and to distract him from the possibility and necessity of altering it. Thus, for Marx, Hegel advocates thought as opposed to activity. There is, however, at least one respect in which we may doubt whether Marx's account is objective. If we examine *The Philosophy of History* in particular, we cannot fail to see the tremendous importance which Hegel attributes to social change. Moreover, the language Marx employs in his critique, saying that everything becomes for Hegel a moment in the life of spirit, distorts Hegel on one essential point. There is no topic in any part of Hegel's system which is seen as arising from any other source than man's own activity. If we dwell only on the theme of the passage of spirit into its otherness in the world and of its return to itself as absolute spirit, we shall have made of Hegel the same type of poetry and metaphor which he himself shows up in, for example, his critique of primitive religions. We shall have made the movement of the spirit, which Hegel uses as a principle of explanation of what men have done in the real world, into some kind of super-human process which lives men's lives for them. Indeed, so strong is Hegel's emphasis on *man* as the maker of history that it is still a matter of controversy whether he recognised the existence of any being outside man, such as God. On this point, Findlay argues that 'Hegel believes in no God and no Absolute except one that is revealed and known in certain experiences of individual human beings, to whose being it is essential to be so revealed and known.'[139]

Findlay equally argues against the notion that Hegel was an anti-empiricist, that he interpreted reality in terms of his own categories rather than on the basis of empirical discovery.[140] On this point, we would first of all note Hegel's profound respect for the autonomy of the natural sciences, as witnessed in his arguments in *The Philosophy of Nature*.[141] While much of what Hegel has to say may nowadays appear quite unscientific, this does not prove that his intention was *anti*-scientific. Throughout his writings on history and social life, as well as in his works on natural science, his standpoint is one of arguing from what he believes to be the facts.

We could go on indefinitely reviewing the complexity and the variations of nuance which can be found in Hegel's philosophy. Here, however, it will be enough to make some points about Marx's interpretation. The very fact that so many different and often opposed trends in philosophy have developed from Hegel is itself an indication that we should beware of so cursory a summary as that which Marx presents. There can be no doubt that while Hegel is answering a different question from Marx's question as to how the world can be changed by man's activity, nevertheless human activity and social change are elements without which Hegel's account would be meaningless. The crucial and absolute choice between thought and activity, which is essential to Marx's interpretation, is not one which Hegel would see as the most important concern of the philosopher. This does not mean that he elevated thought to some realm in which activity was forgotten; it arises simply from the fact that Hegel wanted to express all the dimensions of man's experience, in which thought and activity would be equally valid elements.

As regards the basic misconceptions which Marx attacks in Hegel, I would suggest that his account is less than fair. If consciousness is the sole defining characteristic of man, then Hegel would be forced to regard as inexplicable his activity in the real world. What is the significance of the Unhappy Consciousness if it is not precisely the state in which man is locked in the prison of his own subjectivity? How does he escape from this prison, if not by creating through his own activity an objective social order which will satisfy the need of his essential being to express itself in the world? How does man come to be himself except by creating objective institutions such as the family, without which he is condemned to remain in that narrow subjectivity and primitiveness in which we meet him at the start of *The Philosophy of Right*? How can the objective world be something essentially unimportant if man's becoming himself requires the creation of objective institutions in which to express his essential being?

It must be admitted that all these arguments against Marx's criticisms tend to redress the balance in favour of Hegel to an extent which it would be difficult to defend absolutely. The point I wish to make, however, is that Marx assesses the whole of Hegel's philosophy in the light of a question which Hegel would see as only *one* of the important questions. Marx takes up Hegel on the question of whether he affirms or denies the political situation of early nineteenth-century Germany. Marx's objection to Hegel is in fact, a *political* objection, as Lukàcs points out.[142] In this respect, it would be foolish to deny the truth of Marx's criticisms. Throughout the whole of *The Philosophy of Right*, there is an implicit assumption that man can find his fulfilment in a political state which exists as the unifying principle of civil society. Hegel's philosophy does not go on to extend the democratic ideal beyond the horizons of such a society, as we have seen Marx do in Chapter 2. There is little point in arguing, as does Popitz, that Hegel initially took a far more tolerant attitude to events such as the French Revolution than that which emerges in his later works.[143] In Hegel's last statement on political questions, *The Philosophy of Right*, there is no hint of the possibility that the objective conditions of political life are so intolerable as to require revolution rather than interpretation. Hegel thus, in his explicit political doctrines, fails to affirm the necessity of man's establishing an alternative social universe. As this is precisely the question which Marx is posing, he is quite entitled to be dissatisfied with Hegel's answer to it.

Ultimately, any critique of a philosopher or of a philosophical system is no more and no less valid than the notion of the nature and function of philosophy which underlies it. As we shall see in Chapter 7 there are great and unique merits in Marx's emphasis on social change as the task and main concern of philosophy. Equally, as we shall also see in that chapter, there are elements in Hegel's conception of philosophy that Marx rejects, the rejection of which might be seen as a defect in his own philosophy of the human condition.

Thus Marx's notion of philosophy provides him with the justification for his criticism of Hegel's political stance, but he is led by that criticism to overstress the 'idealism' of Hegel's general philosophy. His criticism of Hegel has all the strengths and all the weaknesses of his notion of what philosophy is about, just as Hegel's own system has the merits and defects of his own notion on the same topic.

I have given much length to a discussion of the importance of social change in Marx's philosophy primarily so as to make clear the reasons for his rejection of Hegel. It is not implied that anyone who disagrees with Marx as to the nature and purpose of philosophy must necessarily reject all his philosophical statements. With this in mind, we may close the present chapter by noting two important aspects of Marx's philosophy which emerge in his criticism of Hegel. Our concern in this study is primarily to see the development of Marx's own ideas, and we should not allow the question of his attitude to Hegel to divert our attention from the development in those ideas which emerges in the essay which we have discussed in this chapter.

The first such development is that of the notion of man as an objective being. Friedrich stresses the importance of this notion as the main point of difference between Hegel and Marx: 'The central aspect of the critique of Hegel is the concept of objectivity.'[144]

In Chapter 4 we considered Marx's notion of the different modes of human activity, and we saw that all these modes involve an interaction of objectification and appropriation. In the present chapter, Marx has deepened the notion of objectification and shown how central it is to his philosophy of man, at a more profound level of philosophical discussion than that on which the discussion in Chapter 4 is conducted.

The second development of Marx's ideas which emerges from this chapter was, as we noted, implicit in Chapter 1. This development is Marx's continued search for a critical stance which will both posit the real status of the world in which we live and assert our freedom to change that world. He has thus far made clear his objections to the idealist stance. In Chapter 6 we shall see how he also rejects materialism, and analyse the notion of praxis, which is the name Marx gives to what he considers an acceptable stance.

6

Some Basic Elements of Marx's Philosophy: Knowledge, Praxis, History

Time present is a cataract whose force
Breaks down the banks even at its source
And history forming in our hand's
Not plasticine but roaring sands,
Yet we must swing it to its final course.

JOHN CORNFORD, *Full Moon at Tierz:
Before the Storming of Huesca*

INTRODUCTION

The task of exposition is now concluded. There remain two important areas of discussion in relation to the Paris writings. One of these is the discussion and evaluation of Marx's philosophy of man at this stage of his development: what picture does he present of the meaning of being human, of the limitations and possibilities of human experience? Is this a convincing and adequate picture? These questions will arise in the next chapter. The other area of discussion, which will concern us in this present chapter, covers some problems of the interpretation of Marx's philosophy: topics on which either his own formulations have been obscure, or there has been controversy produced by misunderstanding, or both.

Three such topics are Marx's theories of knowledge, of praxis and of history. In all three cases there arise the issues of what role and effectiveness Marx accorded to human consciousness, and what freedom he accorded to human activity in history. That Marx's views on these topics are central to his argument in the *Essays and EPM* is beyond doubt: he criticises Hegel for his views on knowledge;[145] he attacks the Practical and Theoretical Parties for their failure to understand the correct relationship of theory to practice;[146] he undermines the methodology of the economists by his insistence on the historical status of economic reality and of their theories about it.[147] If there are problems about Marx's position on these topics, no discussion of the Paris writings can be complete without taking them into account.

But such a discussion, if it is going to give a full account of the questions involved, cannot confine itself to the *Essays and EPM*. This is so for two reasons. In the first place we have theories, such as that of praxis, which are hinted at and implied, but not yet systematically elaborated, in the *Essays and EPM*. In the case of praxis, there is no elaboration until the *Theses on Feuerbach* of 1845 and *The German Ideology* of 1846. In the second place there are theories such as Marx's notion of history, which appear fairly unambiguous and unproblematic if viewed solely from the point of view of the Paris writings, but which give rise to difficulties and controversy when viewed in the context of the other pre-1848 writings. It is only when we view Marx's notion of history, as we come across it in the *Essays and EPM*, in the light of certain passages in *The German Ideology* and in *The Poverty of Philosophy* of 1847 that we can see and attempt to resolve the difficulties to which it gives rise.

It is for these two reasons, in the first place of continuity, and in the second of at least apparent contradiction, between the Paris writings and other pre-1848 works, that these latter are regarded as an integral element in the present discussion. To use 1848 as a watershed is, as the Preface to this work has already argued, not merely arbitrary: the intention of the work is to expound and analyse the *Essays and EPM* in the context of Marx's early writings. Reference will be made both to post-1848 writings and to commentators who base their interpretations largely or even exclusively on these later works, where this appears to be relevant. But the chief purpose of this analysis remains to discuss certain questions in the context of the early works; suggestions as to apparent continuity or conflict between these and the later writings must be taken as no more than suggestions.

EPISTEMOLOGY

The most basic question which arises in any treatment of the relation of human thought to the world is the question of the genesis of human thought itself. The question, how does man come to know? must precede the question, how does man's knowledge relate to the world?

Here, however, we face a problem. Bottomore and Rubel argue that: '[Marx] was not concerned either with the onto-logical problem of the relation of thought and being, or with problems of the theory of knowledge. Speculative philosophy of this kind Marx rejected, in order to substitute science for metaphysics.'[148] This formulation, while somewhat extreme, contains much truth. We have already noted, particularly in Chapter 5, that for Marx every other concern paled in com-parison with the great central question of how to change the world. He was not the kind of philosopher who could take up some isolated question, such as the nature of 'X', or the process of 'X', and be content to discuss it in itself, in its own right. He would always ask himself what was the relation of 'X' to the problem of changing the real world in which men live, and discuss it only under that aspect. The question of epistemology is one which he would refuse to discuss in isolation. This is clear from the essay discussed in Chapter 5, in which we saw that Marx rejected Hegel's standpoint regarding objectivity and the relation of the human subject to it, not because he disagreed with it on 'abstract, philosophical' grounds, but precisely because it inspired an unacceptable solution to the problem of social change.

As this last point would suggest, however, Marx must have had at least implicit positions on many of these 'abstract, isolated' topics, if he was able to reject certain solutions as incorrect on the criterion of their relation to the central problem which concerned him. In other words, although he clearly eschewed discussion of epistemological and other similar topics in their own right, this does not mean that *any* epistemology will accord equally well with his outlook on other questions. It is, in fact, beyond doubt that certain answers to epistemological questions, as for example the Hegelian solution which we have already seen him reject, do not accord with his outlook. What I shall do here is suggest aspects of the unformulated epistemological position which would seem to be necessarily implied by his attitude on other questions that he considered to be of greater importance.

Here Marx's guiding principle, as elsewhere, is that man has made, and therefore can 're-make', can alter and improve, the world in which he lives. Thus the main question which he would pose to any epistemology would ask how it situates the human agent in relation to the world of objects, whether it makes him its master or its slave. Livergood's emphasis on human activity as the central category in elucidating Marxian epistemology is of great relevance here.[149]

Marx gives us a clue to what he would consider a satisfactory position when he opposes what he calls 'naturalism or humanism' to both idealism and materialism.[150] We must ask ourselves why these two latter positions are incorrect on Marx's criteria, and in this way we may arrive at some of the characteristics of a more satisfactory position. For Marx, Hegel's idealism, as we have seen throughout Chapter 5, has both a merit and a defect. Its merit is that it grasps the fact that *the world is a product of man*, in the sense that the objects confronting man are merely instantiations of forms of thought, which latter is man's essential characteristic. Its defect lies precisely in the *sense* in which it sees the world as a product of man. Hegel's world, Marx alleges, is a world of *thought*, man's activity in it is an 'activity' of thought. Human activity thus consists in knowing the world, not in acting upon it. Thus the idealist position is ultimately defective in that it fails to posit the real, empirical world as the medium in which man comes to be. It is thus, for Marx, a flight from reality.

This defect is corrected by the materialist position which, instead of deriving reality from thought, derives thought from reality. Unlike Hegel, it posits the real world as the essential reality, and thus correctly locates the medium in which man really lives. In the essay discussed in Chapter 5, Marx is concerned primarily to reject idealism, and does not give the full basis for the simultaneous rejection of materialism.[151] This is given explicitly in the *Theses on Feuerbach*. In Chapter 5 we saw that Feuerbach's merit was that he corrected the idealist position by the re-assertion of the real empirical world. In the *Theses* we see that Feuerbach has done only half the job:

He does not understand human activity itself as objective activity. . . . The materialist doctrine concerning the changing of circumstances and education forgets that circumstances are changed by men and that the educator must himself be educated. . . . Feuerbach, not satisfied with *abstract thought*, wants *empirical observation*, but he does not conceive the sensible world as *practical*, human sense activity.[152]

9

Thus Feuerbach has certainly done a great service in re-asserting the claims of the real world as against the idealist thought-world. He has, however, in company with the other materialists, asserted a real world which is independent of the human agent, which stands over against and imprisons man.

Hence, in opposition to materialism, the active side was developed by idealism, which of course, does not know real sense activity as such.[153]

The criteria for a correct position may now be clearly seen:
(*a*) Man must not be projected, as pure consciousness, into a world of pure thought, without regard to the fact that he lives and must live his life in the real, empirical world.
(*b*) Equally, with man located in the real world, he must be recognised as its creator, its master, rather than as its prisoner. '[Marx] urged a synthesis that would integrate sensuousness as projected by materialism and activity as projected by idealism.'[154]

Kolakowski, basing his argument mainly on the *EPM*, elaborates an epistemology which fulfils these criteria.[155] The result is something very close to what we would now call critical realism, where account is taken both of the fact that objects are the product of the human agent, and of the fact that these objects have a status in themselves, and are not mere 'thought forms' or products of consciousness. He shows the opposition between such an epistemology and all forms of *reflectionism*. This latter term signifies all epistemological theories which conceive human cognition as the mere reflection in a passive knower of a reality outside that knower. It is precisely for its reflectionism that Marx rejects materialism. Kolakowski argues that 'nascent Marxism formulated a germinal project for a theory of cognition that . . . was replaced by the radically different concepts of Engels and later Lenin.'[156]

It is not within the scope of this work to decide whether Marx himself did or did not move in the direction of that variety of materialist reflectionism elaborated by Engels and Lenin; the decisive texts come well after those which are here our concern. There are however three points which we must note. Firstly, Marx never again was to tackle 'philosophical' questions as explicitly and as profoundly as he did in the early writings. It is thus a possibility that he did not so much 'change his mind' on such questions as simply not return to them. Secondly, there is the interesting point made by Kwant, to the effect that while Marx was quite well aware of the aspects which he opposed in idealism (which of course, because of the prevalence of the Hegelian school, was a far more dangerous enemy than materialism), he lacked the necessary philosophical sophistication to state this opposition while all the time steering away from the obvious alternative of materialism.[157] On this point, Calvez, Copleston and others argue strongly that Marx throughout his life at most remained in a tension between a position such as Kolakowski outlines, and a reflectionist materialism propounded by Engels and, later, Lenin.[158] Thirdly, and most relevant to our discussion, is the fact that at least in the period up to 1848 he had not taken up a dogmatic position on the relation of consciousness to the world, as we shall see in the remainder of this chapter.

Thought and Actuality

Moving away somewhat from the epistemological question as such, but continuing the discussion of the relation of thought and reality, we come to the vital question of whether there is any sense in which thought can function independently of actuality.

In Chapter 2, we saw Marx's discussion of the actuality of contemporary Germany. In that discussion, Marx clearly accepted that there was in Germany a form of thought, called German Philosophy, which was not a direct reflection of the actuality of German life. Nor did he suggest that it was a reflex product of the actuality of other more advanced nations, because he stated that it was not only up to date with, but in some respects *ahead of*, the experience of those nations.[159] A similar point is made in the essay on Hegel discussed in Chapter 5, where Marx recognises that many of the elements of a correct critique are contained in Hegel's thought, the defect lying mainly in how Hegel conceived the nature and function of the critique.[160] Without scoring futile debating points, we may also note that the very intensity and duration of Marx's polemic against his contemporaries and their ideas is ample evidence that he realised that any given actual situation would not give rise automatically to one single thought or set of thoughts. Thus we see that he accepted not only that there was a sense in which thought could outrun actuality, but also that it could do so in more than a single, pre-determined direction.

That these opinions are not mere transient aberrations is shown by the occurrence of a similar argument in *The German Ideology*, where he says that:

if the material elements of a complete revolution are not present . . . then, as far as practical development is concerned it is absolutely immaterial whether the *idea* of this revolution has been expressed a hundred times already.[161]

These points support Tillich's argument that, for Marx 'philosophy anticipates human essentiality, which gains actuality only in the proletarian revolution.'[162] In this context we see the importance of a point made in Chapter 5. There I interpreted Marx's rejection of Hegel as a rejection of the idealist monism which makes thought the sole ultimate reality for man. As our section on epistemology in this chapter has shown, he similarly rejects the materialism which would make the real, empirical world the sole reality. The conclusion to be drawn is that Marx is unwilling to accept *either* monism; for him both thought and actuality are equal, separate and authentic aspects of the human condition, and neither must be subsumed in the other. There is not a *single* reality of thought or actuality, but a *dialectic* of the two. To reverse, in this context, an argument which Marx makes himself: 'thought and being indeed form a unity, but they are also *distinct*' (see B 158). As Rotenstreich points out: 'the very fact that it can transcend reality critically implies, at least, that consciousness is partially independent.'[163]

The concern of this short section has been simply to show that Marx starts off with an acceptance of the equal 'reality' of thought and actuality, that he does not want to reduce either to the other. These two terms will be the theme of the remaining topics of this chapter. The discussion of praxis will elucidate some aspects of what Marx held to be the ideal, the norm of the relationship between the two. The discussion of history and freedom is, in one respect at least, a discussion of the limitations imposed on human praxis by man's historical condition.

PRAXIS

Having established the reality both of thought and of actuality, Marx now proceeds to define the norm for the relation of the two. In doing so he uses the word 'praxis'. This was first introduced into modern criticism by August von Cieszkowski, a Pole, who studied with the Berlin Young Hegelians, and also visited Paris in the 1830s. In 1838 he published his *Prolegomena zur Historiosophie*, in which he made points about Hegelian philosophy which are not unfamiliar to any reader of Marx's own criticisms. He argued that in Hegel, philosophy had reached its highest point, and that the problem of realising it in actuality was not a 'philosophical' problem that could be solved by further philosophical speculation, but rather a problem concerning the nature and function of philosophy itself. What was now required was to realise the *ideas* of philosophy through *action*. 'The future role of philosophy was "to become a practical philosophy or rather a philosophy of practical activity, of 'praxis', exercising a direct influence on social life and developing the future in the realm of concrete activity". This would mean, Cieszkowski claimed, that future history would be one of acts and not of facts.'[164]

Let us review briefly the development of the main elements of Marx's theory of praxis, up to their formulation in the *Theses on Feuerbach*.

(*a*) We have seen in Chapter 1 that Marx, confronting the contrast between German philosophy and German actuality, rejects both the Practical and the Theoretical Parties. He wants a solution in which philosophy will be 'abolished' only in the sense that it will have been shunted into actuality by action. For philosophy to be *accurate*, it must be informed from its inception by the elements of real life in the real world. For philosophy to be *effective*, it must issue in and inform a practice which will bring the real world into line with its ideas.

(*b*) The most important feature of the real world by which philosophical criticism must be informed is the existence of the proletariat, the mass of suffering humanity. As Lukàcs shows, it is on the issue of the proletarian revolution that Marx finally parts company with Bruno Bauer and *Die Freien* at

Berlin.[165] In Chapter 5 we have seen his castigation of these thinkers for their indifference to 'the masses'.[166] It is because their critical attitude is one of pure activity-in-thought, in sublime contempt of the real world, that they are literally incapable of even perceiving the existence of these masses, or their significance as a revolutionary proletariat. Lukàcs shows how at one and the same time Marx opposes to the Young Hegelians both a new approach to criticism and a new object of criticism: 'Critique must necessarily have the effect of mobilising the suffering, oppressed masses, it must inflame them to a revolutionary overthrow of this inverted world.'[167] Without the correct approach we cannot perceive the real object of critique.

(c) At the stage of the essay on Hegel in Chapter 5, we are no longer concerned simply with how to discover the facts correctly, but also with how our discovery can issue in an effective practice to change the world. At this stage the correct stance is outlined chiefly by the negation of incorrect stances. We see that one feature of this correct stance will be that it will neither subsume actuality in thought nor the reverse. Thus, it is implied, the correct position will be found by establishing the correct *relation* between the two realities, thought and actuality.

(d) Finally, this correct relation is specified in the *Theses on Feuerbach*. We have already seen some of the ideas which Marx presents in those theses, in our section on epistemology, and these are all relevant here. There is also a further aspect to the matter. 'The question whether human thinking can pretend to objective truth is not a theoretical but a *practical* question. Man must prove the truth, i.e. the reality and power, the "this-sidedness", of his thinking in practice. The dispute over the reality or non-reality of thinking that is isolated from practice is a purely *scholastic* question.'[168]

Thus praxis is not the grave but the testing-ground of ideas. Marx, in propounding the notion of praxis, is not concerned primarily with the question of whether thought or actuality are 'real' or not. He is not trying, to put it in the crudest terms, to prove to any person that his ideas, no matter how strange or utopian, do not 'exist', cannot be adverted to by consciousness. He *is* saying that only that thought which (a) correctly identifies the problems of the world in which men live their lives, and (*b*) issues in practice which will grapple with those problems, can hope to have any effect on the world. That he is not concerned to attack the reality of thought as such is illustrated by his Husserlian 'bracketing-off' of the 'scholastic' question of whether thought unrelated to activity is real. He neither asserts nor denies that this is so; it is less-than-marginal to his objective, which is not to interpret, but to change, the world.

Thus I would suggest that praxis is best understood as *the specification of the normative relation between thought and practice within the context of the problem of effecting social change*. The use of the word 'normative' here is of the essence. Praxis will not occur without two conscious decisions. It requires (*a*) the decision to adopt the correct attitude in our inquiry as to what are the facts, and (*b*) the decision to carry our knowledge of the facts through into a practice designed to change the world. It requires both critical commitment and, subsequently, revolutionary commitment. Praxis is a norm, not a mechanism. It occurs through decision and commitment, not as the result of some impersonal force against which the critic is powerless. Like virtue, the notion of praxis would be meaningless were there not ample and attractive alternatives. Delfgaauw is justified in his statement that 'the characteristic of Marx's praxis is not that it is action as opposed to thinking, but that it is action based on thinking.'[169]

This section can best be closed with Rotenstreich's rather Chestertonian statement to the effect that 'Marx eliminated philosophy because he took it seriously; he called for life impregnated with philosophy.'[170]

HISTORY

Throughout this study we have seen the great importance of the notion of history in Marx's ideas. In Chapter 2 we saw the analysis of the contemporary social situation, not as a static datum for analysis, but as a stage in the progression of human history. This point emerged most clearly, perhaps, in Marx's analysis of the political revolution and its impact on the feudal polity as world-historical events. In Chapter 3 we considered his earliest model of the economy, and noted that he differed from the economists in that he put economic phenomena and propositions in a historico-humanist context. In Chapter 5 we noted Marx's argument that the merit of Hegel's philosophy lies in its having grasped the fact that the modern world is a creation of human history. We now come to a discussion of some aspects of Marx's notion of history, and particularly of some of the problems arising from it.

History as the ground of freedom: In Chapter 3 we have already seen that it is only because Marx sees the phenomena with which economics deals as products of human history, rather than of the timeless and unalterable laws of the economists, that he can assert the possibility of man's freeing himself from his present economic situation. We need not rehearse the argument here. What is of importance is that for Marx the essential ground of man's freedom in the world is the historicity of that world. If the objective conditions of the present were the product of anything else but man's own activity in history, then there could be no freedom to alter the world. It is thus clear that one of the essential functions of Marx's notion of history is to establish the fact that the objective conditions of the present are not eternal and immutable. In *The Poverty of Philosophy* of 1847 this connection between historicity and freedom is developed. Marx attacks Proudhon's acceptance of the idea that there are eternal economic laws and unalterable economic phenomena:

to get to the bottom of all these questions—what is this but to draw up the real, profane history of men in every century and to present these men as the authors and actors of their own drama? But the moment you present men as the authors and actors of their own history, you arrive—by a detour—at the real starting-point, because you have abandoned those eternal principles of which you spoke at the outset.[171]

History accorded a super-human status: It is significant that in the very same work which contains the above quotation, Marx's notion of history acquires some features which raise doubts in our minds as to whether it does not destroy rather than ground human freedom. History emerges as an entity in itself, with its own internal dynamic, increasingly estranged, it seems, from human agency. For example, we are told that if one were to adopt an a-historical starting-point such as

Proudhon's, 'one would have set oneself the absurd task of eliminating history.'[172]

Economic forces seen as the dynamic of history: Not only this, but the dynamic of history is specified in what is known as the theory of economic determinism. To state this theory at its most extreme, for purposes of discussion, would be as follows. Everything which happens in history is the result of the movement of the economic base of societies. Other elements in the structure of the society, such as the various forms of thought (or 'ideologies') are but reflections of this real movement, and have no reality, no power, in themselves.

In attempting to decide whether this is an adequate formulation of Marx's ideas, we should first advert to the kind of theory which he was trying to discredit when he elaborated his own notions. He draws a not totally unjustified caricature of Proudhon's theory, which he represents as proposing that the dominant force in history is ideas, of which concrete events are merely the expression. Marx argues against this theory, to the effect that:

economic categories are only the theoretical expressions, the abstractions, of the social relations of production. . . . The handmill gives you society with the feudal lord; the steam-mill, society with the industrial capitalist.[173]

There is thus a profound similarity of intention behind the theories both of praxis and of history. Both are designed to refute the belief that the world is governed by mere ideas, and to draw our attention to the real conditions of life. This similarity, however, is far from solving our problem. This is precisely because in his theory of history Marx appears to remove from consciousness much of the reality and freedom which he was prepared to grant it in the theory of praxis. He tells us, for example, that:

The phantoms formed in the human brain are necessarily the sublimates of the material life-process, which is empirically verifiable and bound to material premises.[174]

Contradiction between praxis and history: It is here that we see the relevance of the *Essays and EPM* to any attempt to discuss the problem of Marx's determinism. We have seen how, in those works, the idea of praxis develops. We have seen how it involves the premise that consciousness is not 'unreal', that it is a valid dimension of human reality. It is chiefly in the light of this premise that Marx's determinism becomes a problem. If we had no reason to believe that Marx allowed for the reality and 'activity' of consciousness, then we would have little reason to doubt that he was a crude determinist, holding to a view such as we have sketched above. Several commentators have underlined this point.

Copleston points out that a crude determinist notion of history, denying the reality of all but the economic base, 'could scarcely fit in with Marx's insistence on the unity of theory and practice and on the need for the active preparation of the proletariat's revolutionary overthrow of the capitalist economy.'[175]

Erich Fromm claims that 'Marx actually took a firm stand *against* a philosophical materialism which . . . claimed that "the" substratum of all mental and spiritual phenomena was to be found in matter and material processes.'[176]

Moreover, Fromm illustrates perfectly the tension between the notions of praxis and of history by his argument that the third thesis on Feuerbach[177] 'should make it clear how erroneous it is to interpret Marx as if he, like many philosophers of the enlightenment and many sociologists of today, gave man a passive role in the historical process, as if he saw him as the passive object of circumstances.'[178]

We could multiply the list of such arguments, but have given enough to show that they have two common features. Firstly, they all see an apparent contradiction between Marx's notions of history and of praxis on the question of the reality and freedom of consciousness. Secondly, with due respect to their authors, they tend rather to see than to solve this contradiction. The general line is to say that if Marx said X about praxis he could not consistently have said Y about history: there is little attempt to find out whether he did or did not say Y; these arguments are thus more negative than positive.

Attempts to resolve the contradiction: There are, however, some commentators who do more than note the problem, and who propose methods of solving it.

Kamenka argues that 'what accounts for much of the confusion surrounding the materialist interpretation of history

is Marx's inadequate view of causality—his consistent tendency
to think of causality in general as the production of an effect
by a *single cause* which is by itself both necessary and sufficient
for the effect. . . . The important insight underlying the
materialist interpretation of history has been obscured by the
causal formulation Marx tended to give his doctrine.'[179]

On such a theory of causation, Kamenka argues, Marx had
to find *one direct cause* for all the elements of a society not
included in the term 'economic base', and thus had to conclude
that, for example, mental life is directly 'produced' by that
base. Kamenka proposes an alternative notion of causation.
He would see society as a field of reciprocally interacting
elements (economic base, mental life etc.). We cannot say
that the thought of this society is directly a 'product' of its
economic base. Any change in the latter will have an unpre-
dictable effect, because the ordering of the other elements in
the field will have an influence on the outcome. Some particular
ordering of this field would, for example, mean that the handmill would give us the feudal lord; on the other hand, a
different ordering might not. Kamenka supports his case by
saying that: 'nowhere does Marx show in detail that the
structure or content of any ideology is wholly determined by
the economic conditions or social structure of the group or
society that gave it birth.'[180]

There is a similarity, and also an important difference,
between this thesis and that proposed by Alfred Meyer. Meyer
argues, in agreement with Kamenka, against the 'naïve' causal
interpretation. Meyer, however, rather than proposing an
alternative form *of* causation, proposes an alternative *to*
causation. He is further different from Kamenka in claiming
that Marx in fact gives evidence of not holding dogmatically
to the 'naïve' view. Where Kamenka tells us what it would be
better for Marx to have said, Meyer claims that Marx did in
fact, at least on some occasions, express an alternative to the
'naïve' viewpoint. He says that Marx's interpretation of
history contains many elements of functional thinking: 'Function is a concept denoting mutual dependence of two or more
variables. In functional relationships, a change in any one
variable conditions a change in the other variables.'[181]

Let us take a set of five terms, $T(i) \ldots T(v)$, between which there is a functional relationship. In such a set of terms, we cannot state that any change in the ordering of the terms is the direct result of a change in any one of them. Any such change in one term will have to undergo the modifications exercised by all the other terms. What is of interest here is that all of these terms are active, in the sense that all of them are capable of varying so as to modify the complex ordering of the whole set. Meyer opposes this notion to what he calls the mechanistic notion: 'the functional system consists of variables that change together—reciprocally interdependent variables; the mechanistic system consists of constants that enter into one-sided relationships with other individual "atoms", as causes or effects within the totality of parts.'[182]

On Meyer's interpretation of Marx, it would be meaningless to speak of the 'production' of consciousness by the economic base. We would not speak of the 'cause' of consciousness, but rather of the relationship between it, as an element, a term in the social complex, and the economic base as another term: 'this view is little concerned with cause-and-effect relationships, just as the interdependent variables of mathematical functions are not related to each other as causes and effects.'[183]

Meyer gives evidence for his case that this interpretation is in fact faithful to Marx's own ideas.[184] He deals with the argument that Don Quixote 'could not happen' in a modern economy. He sees this argument as meaning the following: 'according to the Marxist view, the substructure does not create its superstructure; it merely predisposes the society to accommodate the development of superstructural features that are in tune with the substructure. . . . Thus Marxism points out that a Don Quixote cannot possibly thrive in the modern age.'[185]

The terms 'substructure' and 'superstructure' correspond here with what we have called respectively the economic base and the other elements of society. Meyer sees Marx as saying that, even when knight-errantry did exist, it was not a 'product' of the economic base of the times. It was, however, related to that base in that the base was one which made the existence and survival of knights-errant more likely than the existence and survival of, for example, John D. Rockefeller.

Another solution to the problem is that proposed by Louis

Althusser.[186] Althusser's thesis is based on a close examination of the precise reasons for Marx's rejection of Hegel's notion of history. We may very often assume that Marx rejects this notion *simply* because it presents thought as being the central principle governing the movement of human history, and that Marx then substitutes some such term as the economic base in the place of thought. This, Althusser argues, is but half the story. Marx does not simply reject the internal principle of Hegel's system; he rejects the very idea of any system based on a single internal principle: 'The simplicity of the Hegelian contradiction is made possible only by the simplicity of the internal principle constituting the essence of any historical period. ... The reduction of *all* the elements that make up the concrete life of an historical epoch (economic, social, political and legal institutions, customs, morals, art, religion, philosophy and even historical *events*: wars, battles, defeats etc.) to *one* principle of internal unity, is only possible on the absolute condition of taking the whole concrete life of a people for the exteriorisation-alienation of an internal spiritual principle.'[187]

Althusser thus argues that were we to interpret Marx as proposing a materialist determinism, we would be seeing the difference of the Hegelian and Marxian systems as one simply of principle, and not also of form. He argues that Marx's system differs from Hegel's in form, in that every historical event for Marx is the result of a situation which is not 'simple' but 'over-determined'. This means that all the elements of the society must be taken into account if we are to understand history, and the specific role and weight of each must be assessed. Interestingly enough, Althusser refers explicitly to the argument about the handmill and the steam-mill, which I have already quoted. He argues that we must not interpret this to mean that the material economic base 'produces' the feudal lord; if we do so, we are making of Marx's ideas a system with one single internal principle of movement, and getting the 'mirror image' of the Hegelian idealist system. Althusser says that this particular argument of Marx's is often taken out of context. Let us see this context. After the passage about the handmill, Marx goes on to say that

the same men who *establish* their social relations in conformity with their material productivity, *produce* also principles, ideas and categories, in conformity with their social relations.[188]

I have emphasised the verbs in this quotation to stress the point that man here is seen as himself producing all the various dimensions of his social life, and thus is not the prisoner of determination by an economic base. The point which Marx is making here need not involve 'crude' determinism. It can consistently be understood as suggesting that there will be a tendency towards correspondence between all the different elements of the social complex rather than that any one element 'produces' all the others. It is significant that this last quotation is the very passage which Garaudy relies on to support his argument that 'there is no question whatsoever of regarding the superstructures as the "epiphenomena" of production. The relation between these superstructures and production is in no way a mechanical one.'[189]

There is another passage from the *Poverty of Philosophy* which Althusser does not refer to, but which would appear to lend support to his thesis. This is where Marx ridicules Proudhon's attempt to take one single feature of a society in isolation, and to give a convincing account of its genesis and significance without reference to any other element of the society. Marx argues that he cannot do so

without having recourse to all the other relations of society. . . . How indeed could the *single logical formula* of sequence of time, of move-ment explain the structure of society, in which *all relations co-exist simultaneously and support one another?*[190]

The emphasis added to this passage illustrates how it would seem to support Althusser's interpretation of Marx in the two following respects : (i) Marx proposes a view of society as a complex of interdependent relations rather than as a pattern of cause and effect. (ii) He rejects a 'single logical formula'. Althusser quotes from Engels' letter to Bloch, written in 1890, where Engels argues that the economic base is 'determining', but only 'in the last instance. . . . More than this neither Marx nor I have ever asserted. Hence if somebody twists this into saying that the economic element is the *only* determining one, he transforms that proposition into a meaningless, abstract, empty phrase.'[191]

We may summarise and conclude Althusser's thesis by quoting his argument that 'in history . . . the superstructures etc.... are never seen to step aside when their work is done or, when the time comes, as his pure phenomena, to scatter before His Majesty the Economy as he strides along the royal road of the dialectic. From the first moment to the last the lonely hour of the "last instance" never comes.'[192]

Let us conclude this section by noting the similarities between these three attempts to solve the issue of Marx's determinism. All three start from an attack on what they would call a 'naïve, crude' determinism which sees the economic base as 'producing' all the other elements of the social complex. Kamenka argues that Marx himself fell prey to this error. He claims, however, that his basic insight can be expressed correctly only by seeing the economic base as but one term in a *field* of terms, where all the terms will have a role in determining the course of events. Both Meyer and Althusser argue, on the contrary, that it is *we* who err when Marx is interpreted as a 'crude' determinist. They propose interpretations in terms of functional relationships (Meyer) and overdetermination (Althusser). In both these systems the economic base is regarded as the dominant, but not exclusively determining, term in a complex of terms between which there are relations of reciprocal interaction. Both systems, rather than speaking of the 'production' by the economic base of the other elements of the social complex, would speak of a tendency towards correspondence between that base and the other elements.

The degree of historical determination: Our discussion so far has been concerned exclusively with the *nature* of historical determination. There remains the question whether Marx saw the *degree* of that determination as constant in every era of history.

It has emerged throughout this analysis that it is Marx's most profound intention to liberate man from the restrictions and necessity imposed by his present less-than-human situation. In Chapter 2 we saw the rejection of political emancipation on the grounds that it was incomplete, and the implication that a more complete emancipation was possible. In Chapter 4 we saw that Marx proposed modes of activity for the future society which all presupposed the elimination of economic necessity, because 'sense which is subservient to crude needs has only a restricted meaning' (B 161-2). Bigo expresses this point well when he argues that 'Marxist materialism aims precisely at the liberation of man from this economic materialism.'[193]

The relevance of these arguments to the discussion of Marx's historical determinism is as follows: if Marx was (i) concerned with man's liberation from imposed necessity, and also (ii) a determinist in some sense, does this imply that he envisaged that in the future there would be a smaller *degree* of determination than in all previous societies? Marcuse claims that this is so: 'Marx emphasises time and again that his materialistic starting point is forced upon him by the materialistic quality of the society he analyses.'[194]

In Chapter 4 we saw that Marx foresaw the possibility of a reduction of the dominance of the economic pattern by means of automation. Rudi Supek argues that 'the most basic of Marx's assumptions was that the development of science and its application to technology will permit a diminution, a progressive shrinking, of the amount of man's necessary work.'[195]

It is significant that Supek draws his evidence not only from the *EPM*, but also from the later *Grundrisse*.[196] Moreover, as we have already noted,[197] a similar assumption emerges in Marx's latest work, the final volume of *Capital*. In this latter Marx argues that while we have 'freedom' in present circumstances in that we can acquire control over nature:

nevertheless, this always remains a realm of necessity. Beyond it begins that development of human potentiality for its own sake, the true realm of freedom, which however can only flourish upon that realm as its basis. The shortening of the working day is its fundamental pre-requisite.[198]

Behind all these arguments is the assumption, noted in Chapter 4, of a significant difference in the degree of historical determination of man's freedom between all societies within the reign of necessity and the society of the future. Marx suggests elsewhere that the reason for the dominance of the economic pattern over the affairs of men in all historical societies is that

men must be in a position to live in order to be able to 'make history'. But life involves before everything else eating and drinking, a habitation, clothing and many other things. The first historical act is, therefore, the production of material life itself. . . . Today, as thousands of years ago, [it] must be accomplished every day and every hour merely in order to sustain human life.[199]

Once, however, man has developed to the point where this act can be accomplished by technology, the 'first historical act' will no longer exercise the same determining role over his life and thought.

How does this insight accord with the different interpretations of the nature of Marx's determinism? We may say that it accords with the 'crude' interpretation, but only in the sense that it does not directly contradict it. There is, however, a problem. If Marx believes that the elements of man's social life are directly 'produced' by the economic base, what happens when that base declines in importance by the elimination of necessity? We are left with the awful prospect of the disappearance of society at the very hour when it has freed itself from determination by economic necessity. It is as if the dining-room were to vanish into air just when the dinner is cooked.

The alternative interpretations, of which we may take Althusser's as an example, make the change more comprehensible. The abolition of the reign of necessity would mean a fundamental and irreversible re-ordering of the terms of the social complex; the economic base, while not disappearing, would lose its dominant status. The new ordering of the terms could be on either of two different patterns: (a) Some new element of the complex, such as for example 'aesthetic activity' could acquire a dominant status. (b) Alternatively, the new ordering could be such that there would no longer be any dominant term; each dimension of human activity could develop in its own right, without being significantly determined by any other dimension. This latter possibility would seem to accord better than the first with Marx's notion, already noted in Chapter 4, that in the future society man will fulfil himself:

in an all-inclusive way . . . [which will be] just as varied as the determinations of human nature and activity are diverse. (B 159)

I would suggest that the superior ability of the alternatives to the crude determinist interpretation to envisage the transition from the reign of necessity is an argument, although not yet conclusive evidence, in their favour.

10

7

Marx's Philosophy of Man in The Paris Writings

> Marx attempted the *tour de force* of expressing an
> authentic affirmation of man in his essential
> primacy without ever having recourse to ethical
> metaphysical or religious categories.
>
> P. BIGO,
> *Marxisme et Humanisme*

INTRODUCTION

The purpose of this chapter is to give an account and a critical
evaluation of Marx's philosophy of man, his understanding of
the nature and possibilities of human experience as this emerges
in the Paris writings. In this, the notion of species-being will
be crucial, as will be apparent from its featuring at so many
points in earlier chapters. Unlike those earlier discussions, our
purpose here is to draw together the different clues which
Marx scatters throughout the Paris writings, and derive as
full a notion as possible of the meaning of species-being. To
achieve this we must firstly advert to the influence of Feuerbach
on Marx, the importance of which, if not already established
in the reader's mind, will quickly become apparent. Although
this present account is based on the Paris writings as far as
textual references go, the scope of the questions which I
discuss, and of the works of other authors whom I cite or quote,
goes beyond these to the early works in general, and includes
some of the basic philosophical presuppositions of his total
corpus of writings.

FEUERBACH ON MAN AND RELIGION

In Chapters 1, 4 and 5, we have noted the influence of
Feuerbach on Marx's methodology, especially as a counter-
irritant to Hegelian idealism in the development of the notion
of praxis. The works which are most relevant in this respect
are his 'Vorläufige Thesen zur Reformation der Philosophie'

and *Grundsätze der Philosophie der Zukunft*, both published in 1843.[200] But here it is with the earlier work, *Das Wesen Des Christentums*[201] of 1841, that we are concerned chiefly.

In this earlier work, Feuerbach presents man as a species-being. He argues that man has an infinite consciousness, unlike any other creature, and is thus able to conceive of himself not as an isolated unit, but rather as a being whose essence is his species-essence (*Gattungswesen*). Each individual is but a limited, finite member of this species; nevertheless he possesses human attributes such as goodness, wisdom, strength, creativity and so on. Realising that these attributes are in principle infinite, the individual is caught in a contradiction between his own finitude and the inherent infinity of the attributes which he finitely possesses. This he resolves by conferring these attributes on a superhuman being, whom he calls God. In each culture there will be a god, to whom will be assigned those attributes which are uppermost in the consciousnesses of the people of that culture, such as gods of war, of love, of creativity and so forth. If we consider the historical succession of gods, and ask what is common to all of them once we have removed the particular attributes predicated of each, we will be left only with the name 'God'. We will come to realise that: 'the mystery of the inexhaustible fullness of the divine predicates is therefore nothing else than the mystery of human nature.'[202]

In other words, 'God' is merely a formal, contentless name for a succession of combinations of inherently infinite human attributes. These are the attributes of the species, which is capable of realising to their full extent those attributes which each member of the species possesses only in his finitude. Man, the species-being, makes, however, the mistake of predicating of God not only these attributes, but also a real being in and for himself. 'Man—this is the mystery of religion—projects his being into objectivity, and then again makes himself an object to this projected image of himself thus converted into a subject.'[203]

Feuerbach does not call himself an atheist in the accepted sense: 'he alone is the true atheist to whom the *predicates* of the Divine Being are nothing; not he to whom merely the *subject* of these predicates is nothing.'[204] In other words, Feuerbach denies that there is a God, but does not deny the reality for man the species-being of those attributes which he predicates of God. What he asks is that we realise that the species has now come to the point in its maturation where it can see itself as the infinite realisation of the 'Divine' attributes.

I do not claim that this is even an approach to a full treatment of Feuerbach's ideas on this subject.[205] We have, however, isolated two aspects of these ideas which are of central relevance to Marx's subsequent use of the notion of species-being: (i) The notion that man's essence is social, that society can be the realisation of man's being, that the individual can find his complete development, his fulfilment, in a fully developed community. (ii) The notion that, so long as traditional religious consciousness predominates, man lessens himself in proportion as he magnifies God. Everything attributed to God is properly an attribute of man as species-being, and therefore what God gains, man loses. 'For Feuerbach, then, the choice is between man and a God who prevents man from being himself, a God who is a competitor with man.'[206]

We may consider the sequence of Marx's development of this notion in the Paris writings.

Political aspect: Here I use the term 'political' simply to refer to the subject-matter of the *Essays*, thus avoiding the difficulty raised by the rejection of 'political' emancipation and so forth expressed in those works. Marx tells us that man is a species-being. The first point to be noted is that Marx makes this statement in both a static and a dynamic context. As an observation about man's present condition, species-being is presented as man's essential social being, which is in contradiction with his present particular, egoistic mode of existence. Thus Marx makes the observation that the dichotomy of public and private spheres is the division between the sphere in which man has in part expressed his species-being and that in which he remains not-yet-a-species-being. This points to the dynamic context, in which we see that man not only *is* a species-being in contradiction with his present particular and egoistic life, but will also *become* a species-being in a full sense, when such contradictions will no longer exist (see B 13, 31).

Both God and the democratic state are presented here much as Feuerbach presents God. Both are alien entities to which man attributes what he has so far been prevented from realising in himself. God stands not only for the unfulfilled potential of each individual, but also for the community, the transcendence of particularity, which is man's essential being although it has not yet been realised on earth. At a later stage, the state fulfils the same functions, although Marx does not specify whether the state represents the unfulfilled potential of individuals as well as the ideal of community (see B 17, 20, 43–4). Marx's critique of the Rights of Man also develops his notion of species-being, in that he says that when the division of state and civil society, of which division these rights are a symptom and a ratification, has disappeared, each individual will no longer see his own fulfilment as exclusive of that of others and vice versa. Indeed, the fulfilment of each and all will be so intertwined that the distinction itself will no longer be thinkable (see B 24–7).

Economic aspect: When Marx turns to economic analysis, we find that he proposes an empirical basis for the notion of species-being. This basis has already been hinted at by Engels.[207] Marx argues from the fact that the enormous wealth which has been created in the industrial period, and the enormous potential for the creation of new wealth ('wealth' here in the sense of abundance of material necessities) are products of human co-operation, of intelligent organisation of the capacity of the species, rather than of each individual acting in isolation. The species acts upon nature, because the material environment in its unworked-on state is man's inorganic life, the material basis of the development of the species. Although in present conditions it takes place in the alienated situation of labour, the creation of wealth through division of labour is an expression of the capacities of the species (see B 126–9).

Post-economic aspect: In present conditions, one of the greatest barriers to the fulfilment of man as a species-being is the system of appropriation through private property. There is a striking similarity between Marx's rejection of private property and his rejection of the Rights of Man. Both are assessed in relation to man's essential species-being, and are found to be destructive of it in that they posit the fulfilment and self-expression of each person as being exclusive of that of others. Marx proposes new modes of objectification and of appropriation—that is, new modes of activity, in which man's species-being will be fully realised. And here we come to a central point which could be very easily overlooked.

If we do not examine closely what Marx says about man's development as a species-being, we may interpret it simply along the following lines. We may see his rejection of present modes of activity as a rejection of modes of activity in which man is not *social*, in which he acts as an isolated individual in antagonism to his fellows. We may interpret the stage of full species-being as a stage where man will no longer act as such an individual, where he will be other-directed. While all of these points are involved in Marx's thinking, the analysis which we reviewed in Chapter 4 should make us aware of a point which, while difficult to state clearly, is of vital importance. The new modes of activity will differ not only in being social but also in being, from the viewpoint of each individual, qualitatively different and new modes of self-expression. When the species has realised itself in a fully developed community which is no longer merely 'theoretical' (i.e. divorced from men's real lives in the real world), then each person will be doing things and perceiving the world in a different way from the modes of activity proper to every preceding period of history. This difference will lie not only in the fact that these modes of activity will now be those of man in a fully developed community, but also in that they will be the fruit of the liberation of man's capacities for aesthetic experience, genuine interpersonal relations of love, intellectual creativity and so forth from the pattern imposed on all those capacities by the age of necessity. I do not suggest that Marx thinks it possible for man to be active in these modes in any society other than that of fully developed species-being; in other words, the 'sociality' of these new modes is inextricably woven into them, so that we should not attempt, except for purposes of illustration, to speak of the sense in which they are new *as well as* social. The point is raised simply to dispel the understandable but incorrect impression that man when he is a full species-being will be doing much the same things as before but 'in a social kind of way'. The inherent sociality of the new modes of activity derives from the fact that they involve appropriation through a mode other than that of competitive possession.

This being so (for development, see Chapter 4 pp. 73–8) man will fulfil himself in these modes in ways which do not require him to erect barriers against the simultaneous self-fulfilment of others. Indeed, modes of activity will develop whose very essence and objective is sociality; in other words, the value of human contact and community will be pursued for its own sake, a point that Marx derived from his experience of the clubs run by French artisans, where

Their association itself creates a new need—the need for society—and what appeared to be a means has become an end. . . . Society, association, entertainment which also has society as its aim, is sufficient for them; the brotherhood of man is no empty phrase but a reality. (B 176)

Thus we see that Marx does not argue simply that man has a capacity to be social, which he must fulfil. He argues that man cannot fulfil any of his capacities freely except by the fulfilment of his essential being as a member of a community; man's 'social capacity' and all of his 'personal capacities' can develop only together, only in the context of the community of developed species-beings.

When man lives as a species-being in the real, non-theoretical community, his needs will be a motive to self-fulfilment rather than a diminution of himself. This will of course affect his perception of nature. No longer will he approach the material world under the compulsion of necessity, seeing objects under the one generic category of 'things-to-be-possessed'. He will have developed his own capacities to the point where each object will reveal its own specific qualities to him, because he will respond to each with the correct specific faculty, such as the musical ear to music, the educated eye to paintings, and so forth (see B 160–62). Thus man will have humanised the whole natural world. He will no longer suppress the specific qualities of specific components of that world. He will no longer suppress his own faculties by approaching that world as a set of undifferentiated needs which dominate him. In short, he will have become one with nature, because nature will have been made one with man (see B 162–4).

All of these developments are summed up in Marx's impressive pronouncement that communism as a fully developed naturalism is humanism and as a fully developed humanism is naturalism. It is the *definitive* resolution of the antagonism between man and nature, between man and man. It is the true solution of the conflict between existence and essence, between objectifications and self-affirmation, between freedom and necessity, between individual and species. It is the solution of the riddle of history, and knows itself to be this solution. (B 155)

AMBIGUITY OF 'COMMUNISM'

There remains, however, one unsolved problem. Marx tells us that communism is a necessary stage in man's development towards full species-being:

Communism is the necessary form and dynamic principle of the immediate future, *but communism is not itself the goal of human development—the form of human society.* (B 167—my italics)

Does not Marx contradict himself, if we juxtapose this and the preceding quotation? Milligan argues that here Marx is rejecting only *crude* communism, that form of communism which is dominated by the sense of having.[208] Tucker directly opposes this interpretation, and argues that Marx sees man as transcending even developed forms of communism.[209] There is a measure of truth in both arguments. If Milligan means that Marx rejects crude communism because it is a form of the sense of having, then he is correct. If Tucker wishes to lay especial emphasis on the point that, as we have already seen in this chapter, more is involved in truly human activity than a rearrangement, or even an abolition, of property relationships, then he also is justified. The truth is that there is an ambiguity in Marx which, if we understand it, is not a serious problem. When Marx contrasts the future society with the present society based on private property, he tends to speak of communism as the mode of appropriation which will replace this latter. When he speaks of the future society in its own right, however, he is anxious to make it clear that in this future society it will be meaningless to speak of ownership of any kind, whether through private property, or through 'crude' or other forms of communism. To put forward some developed form of communism as an end in itself, as the goal of human development, would be to make the same mistake as negating private property, and we would remain blind to the positive development in human activity to which communism is but the means. Thus the ambiguity is between Marx's use of the term 'communism' in two senses: as (a) the negation of private property (and in general of the sense of having); and as (b) the term for all the various dimensions of truly human activity in the future society. Marx is anxious to make it clear that communism is not an end in itself precisely because if we do not grasp this point we will envisage communism merely in sense (a), and will be no more than 'crude' communists, more aware of our opposition to private property than of the positive developments in human experience for which communism should liberate us. When he says that communism is not itself the goal of human development, he clearly does not mean that there will be some further revolution in human society after the establishment of communism. Thus he *does* see communism as the solution of the riddle of history, but equally wants to make us aware of the creative possibilities for which communism is but the condition, lest the communist revolution be merely one more

phenomenal form of the infamy of private property representing itself as positive community. (B 155)

EVALUATION OF MARX'S PHILOSOPHY OF MAN IN THE PARIS WRITINGS

The contents of this volume so far have been exposition and interpretation of Marx's ideas as these developed during the Paris period. I have already said, however, that we would have little need or justification for analysing these ideas were it not that they presented interesting arguments and insights about important topics. I hope that the book so far will have shown that the Paris writings do indeed possess this intrinsic merit; it now remains to suggest an evaluation of these ideas, an assessment of how they measure up to whatever standard of adequacy we employ in the areas in question.

Philosophical Foundations

We may take it that Marx intends his analysis to be accepted as that of a social scientist, in the sense that he claims to have sought the facts by a rigorous empirical inquiry, and to have empirical evidence on which to base, and if necessary defend, his assertions. There is a large number of questions as to the validity and extent of Marx's scientific analysis, with which I do not intend to deal here. My concern is rather to deal with what I have called his 'philosophy of man', with an aspect of the philosophical foundations of his analysis and prescription. What do I mean by these phrases?

In our dealings with our fellow-actors at the level of common-sense living, or in our discussions with a social scientist, we could conceive of ourselves as uttering the charge: 'But you haven't any basis for saying that: the facts don't warrant your acting in this way in your ordinary living, or drawing this conclusion in your scientific work.' Disagreeing with a person in this manner, I shall call an evidential or scientific disagreement. What is important is that such disagreement presupposes a measure of more fundamental *agreement* as to what will rank as evidence, what are the important questions to be asked, how to tackle the subject-matter in question and so forth. There is however a different kind of criticism which is directed precisely at those fundamental presuppositions which give meaning to evidential or scientific disputes. Examples are where R. D. Laing tells established psychiatry that it has gone wrong not simply in this or that aspect of procedure or calculation, but rather in its entire conception of the nature of and correct approach to mental illness; or where Peter Winch attacks the behaviourists for misconstruing their subject-matter by confusing reasons given for human behaviour with the image of cause adopted in natural science.[210] When we call in question a scientist's very understanding of his field and its proper method, as when we disagree with our fellow-citizens as to the very meaning of words like 'progress', 'liberty' and so forth, our disagreement and challenge are proposed not at the scientific or evidential, but at the philosophical level. We are calling in question the whole horizon within which the other person is working, the horizon which delimits the field of reality for him, and orients him within that field according to certain priorities.

The kind of philosophical question with which I am here concerned is most impressively and concisely indicated by Alasdair MacIntyre, who speaks of Marxism as attempting to offer: 'an interpretation of human existence by means of which men may situate themselves in the world and direct their actions to ends that transcend those offered by their immediate situation.'[211]

Whatever may be the role of transcendence, in one of its many senses, in the Marxian or our own 'interpretation of human existence', it is this question of interpretation and orientation which is at issue when we discuss and assess Marx's philosophy of man.

My method will not display the rigour which would be taken for granted in a discussion of Marx's scientific methodology. My intention is to discuss briefly some at least of the merits of Marx's position in relation to the question of philosophy of man, and then to suggest areas in which developments in the period since he wrote, developments as much in concrete social experience as in specialised philosophy, would indicate deficiencies in his position.

Community

One of the chief strengths of Marx's philosophy of man is his understanding and application of the idea of human community; this is hardly surprising when we consider the centrality of the notion of species-being in the writings which we have examined. I shall not here give any further interpretation of that notion; I would like, however, to assess it as one of the fundamental categories of Marx's interpretation of man. Surely he was not the first philosopher to put forward the ideal of brotherhood, to condemn competition and individualism as immoral? Quite so: his merit is that he put forward his ideal, and criticised present actuality, from an empirical standpoint rare or totally absent in other philosophies of brotherhood. The result is that, as he himself is quite well aware, he is not in the position of those Utopian socialists who sit on the side-lines and make well-nigh contentless statements about 'the brotherhood of man', while quite unable to encompass the given state of affairs and the proposed ideal within a consistent argument. While the ideal of social man as opposed to atomistic individualism may be older than Plato, it was in Marx's hands that this ideal was equipped to grapple with the realities of industrial society. As MacIntyre argues: 'The achievement of Marx [in the *EPM*] is to have given historical form to a concrete view of what man in society ought to be, of what he is, and of how his estrangement from his own true being comes about.'[212]

We have already noted[213] in the discussions of Marx's theory of human activity and of his conception of communist society that the notion of species-being is profoundly personalist in intention:

it is above all necessary to avoid postulating 'society' once again as an abstraction confronting the individual. (B 158)

Crude communism is rejected on the grounds that:

it negates the *personality* of man in every sphere. (B 153)

But the radical personalism of Marx's notion of species-being is best established by referring to his theory of human activity. Here Marx could well be said even to labour the point that species-being, when realised, will not be an abstract, alien social force which will either be imposed on or swallow up the existence and value of each individual person.

If I lived in a society of fully-developed species-beings, this fact would appear as much in the quality of my own experience and activity as a person, as in the quality of my social relations with my fellow-men: indeed, activity and experience can become truly human only when truly social: when such, they will be the activity and experience of truly human and truly social beings. Marx claims[214] that the achievement of a true communist society will break down the assumed unbridgeable gap between atomic individuals and their social structure which lies at the root of at least the post-Hobbesian political ideology of western Europe. We should be careful in assessing his notion of species-being lest we make criticisms which assume that very gap. Perhaps to ask whether person and society will be opposed in communist society is to have our minds closed to the fundamental condition of the realisation of species-being.

History

I have already drawn attention, in Chapter 5, to the centrality of the notion of human history in Marx's thought.[215]

Perhaps the first point which he makes us realise is simply that we *have* a history: neither the conditions of our assurance nor those of our sufferings are unalterable. The world which we inhabit loses its obvious solidity, and becomes, for better or worse, a moment of history. I have used the phrase 'for better or worse', and done so advisedly. We are liberated in reality by the fact, in consciousness by the realisation, that we have a history: but is this not a traumatic liberation? 'Society provides us with warm, reasonable, comfortable caves, in which we can huddle with our fellows, beating on the drums that drown out the howling hyenas of the surrounding darkness. "Ecstasy" is the act of stepping outside the caves, alone, to face the night.'[216]

The point about Marx's insistence on the fact of our historicity is that, unlike for example many existentialist accounts of facticity and contingency, it liberates us not only negatively, away from the meaning of our established social reality, but also positively, in the direction of an attainable really human society. This is the point of my first quotation from MacIntyre above.

But the implications of Marx's notion of human history are not exhausted at this point. We are not entitled, he would argue, to overcome the contingency and limitations of our given, empirical world by dissolving it into, or setting it against, some abstract philosophical notion of 'the meaningful process of history'. As we have already seen in Chapter 5, Marx charges Hegelian philosophy with just this mistake. Marx is in his central inspiration a philosopher of the here and now. He rejects the here and now which he finds, but rejects them not in favour of a timeless and placeless essentialist 'humanity', but in terms of an attainable really human and social here and now. Against the serenity of the Hegelian philosophy, Marx would join the existentialists in saying it is unauthentic to claim to live by values which rest on an abstract and really contentless 'other-world'; such values are an escape from the contingency of history, and also from the claim of a new real history to be made. Marx's philosophy of praxis holds together the themes of historical contingency, historical transcendence and the concrete, real fulfilment of human potentiality. If the balance in which these hang together is precarious, this is a

comment more on the human predicament than on a defect in
Marx's philosophy.

Some Criticisms of this Philosophy

We may now consider and assess some criticisms which
allege that Marx is either incorrect or incomplete in his
philosophical picture of the significance and possibilities of the
human condition.

Perhaps the most important charge made against Marx's
philosophy, at least in the area of socio-political implications,
is that of some brand or other of totalitarianism. Our concern
at this point in the argument is not with actual regimes which
claim the title of Marxism and pursue more or less Stalinist
policies. The question is whether there is a strain, or even a
central current, in Marx's own thinking which suppresses the
fact and value of personality in some political or social collec-
tivity. I shall not rehearse the evidence which I have already
adduced to show not only that Marx did not intend such a
consummation, but that he was very definitely aware of the
need to say that he did not intend it. In *The German Ideology*
of 1846, a work in many senses less 'philosophical' and
'Hegelian' than the Paris writings, he makes the point that
when men do not control their lives humanly, they attribute
a false autonomy and reality-in-itself to their society and
history:

[which appear as] an alien force existing outside them, of the
origin of which they are ignorant, which they thus cannot control,
which on the contrary passes through a peculiar series of stages and
phases independent of the will and the action of man, nay even
being the prime governor of these.[217]

Even though I do not doubt this personalist intention of
Marx's notion of community, I think that there is a number
of inter-related considerations which both point to a deficiency
in Marx's philosophy and add plausibility to the charge of
totalitarianism.

Perhaps the most striking mark of modern philosophical
discussion is the way in which it converges, separated as it is
into different schools and specialised into watertight subject-
areas, on the problem of the philosophy of the person. For

example, the group of philosophers who are called somewhat loosely 'personalist', and would include the group called 'Christian personalists' have been concerned centrally with the case that the rise of positive science has not in fact proved the concept of person to be an 'unnecessary hypothesis' invoked by adolescent humanity; without such a concept we cannot adequately interpret our experience of being human and behaving humanly.[218] The school of 'philosophical psychology', influenced among others by the philosophy of the later Wittgenstein, has shown that we cannot make sense of human behaviour if we do not grasp its 'self-involving' dimension,[219] what one philosopher calls the 'irreducible first-person sense' which permeates our utterances and our actions. The critical realist position of the 'Transcendental Thomists', of whom the central figure is Bernard Lonergan, also makes a fundamental point of allowing for the role of the knowing and acting subject in all areas of philosophy, starting from the role of knowing subject in epistemology.[220]

This list could be greatly extended, but my point has been made. What exactly is my point? I would stress that it is not to suggest a superficial unity of approach between the styles of thought which I have listed: it is rather to draw attention to their common sharing of a *problem* which John MacMurray pinpoints neatly when he says that 'the cultural crisis of the present is indeed a crisis of the personal. But the problem it presents to philosophy is a formal one. It is to discover or to construct the intellectual form of the personal.'[221]

MacMurray develops his thesis. He claims that philosophy has evolved adequate languages for dealing with mathematical problems and problems of organisms, which developments accompanied the development of the mathematical and natural sciences. The real problem now, he says, is to evolve an adequate set of concepts, or in a special sense a language, for expressing and dealing with the personal.

Marx's philosophy is certainly not the place to seek a comprehensive and nuanced philosophy of the human person which will meet contemporary exigencies. But this criticism, if it is to be fair and useful, must be developmental. In other words, it must not make the mistake of blaming Mozart for not having the musical 'vocabulary' of Stravinsky. A phil-

osopher, like an artist or a scientist, inherits a horizon and a
conceptual vocabulary which define and in their turn are
defined by the concerns and experiences of his age. Jean-Paul
Sartre argues strongly that insights into the way in which the
person interacts creatively with his environment are by no
means foreign to an adequate Marxist analysis—indeed, they
are a required dimension of it.[222] But to prove that something
is not foreign to a philosopher's thinking is not to say that he
himself fully understood it and accorded it the correct weight
in his thinking. I believe that it is logically consistent—and
also necessary—to argue both that Marx was personalist in the
intention and even in the formulation of his vision of developed
species-being, and that, largely due to the state of development
of philosophical analysis, we can recognise that he neither
emphasised nor fully grasped the intricacies and dimensions
of what is involved in being a person. Indeed, sociologists like
Peter Berger[223] could be said to be applying to the field of
'micro-sociology', of the interactions of the human person and
his complex, many-levelled social *milieu*, that critical attitude
which Marx pioneered in, but restricted in application to, the
area of 'macro-sociology', of the interactions of human groups
and their actions on the social environment.

But can we attribute this aspect of Marx's thought solely
and simply to the deficiencies of the contemporary philosophical
concerns and equipment? Such an explanation could well be
offered in the case of one or even a few philosophers; if
generalised, it completely fails to grasp or account for the
process of development, an appreciation of which requires that
we recognise the ability at least of some philosophers to
transcend the limitations of the questions and answers which
they inherit. There are, however, additional and specific
reasons for rejecting, in Marx's case, an explanation made
solely in terms of the state of contemporary thought. Was it
not precisely Marx's achievement as a thinker to have broken
through the confines and presuppositions of the intellectual
world in which he found himself? If he could do so with
notions like praxis and species-being, why not with the data
which ground the developments in the philosophy of the
person?

I believe that Marx made a value-judgement, or decision,

about the importance of certain types of question. My evidence
for this is partly a point which I have already made in Chapter
6, about Marx's considering that, for example,

the dispute over the reality or non-reality of thinking which is
isolated from practice is a purely *scholastic* question.[224]

I am not myself concerned at the moment with this particular
question; rather is it my object to point out that it falls in a
certain area of questions which lies about as far as one can get
away from conscious social activity and transformation of the
world. I would suggest that Marx's decision about priorities
would reject such questions for precisely that reason. For
instance, he deals summarily with the questions of creation
and death in a few pages of the *EPM*.[225] I shall not here dwell
on his attitudes to these problems, except to suggest that the
relative ease with which he disposes of them is a result of
factors which help to clarify the aspect of his thought that we
are here trying to explain. I would suggest that Marx's
'bracketing-off' of certain questions is closely related to his
optimism about the feasibility of the project of realising species-
being; a fundamental optimism about the possibility of
realising the ideal society through human endeavour can well
ground an attitude which regards certain fundamental questions as false or irrelevant. If we are optimists about a process
of human history towards a terminus of value, in which
process our lives achieve meaning and value as an effort
towards this consummation, then we may well not attach such
great weight as otherwise to the kinds of ultimate question to
which religion offers an answer. It is when our confidence
about achieving this end is called into question that we will
grasp in their full implications and importance the questions
which we had hitherto understandably rejected.

But however I explain it, am I not inconsistent in making
this observation about an incompleteness in Marx's philosophy
while still claiming that he is a personalist? I do not believe
so, and for the following reasons. Both Marxism and its chief
competitor as a philosophy of man, Christianity, would
envisage a situation in which the antinomy of person and
community will no longer hold, because being a person and
being a member of a community will no longer refer to

11

opposed dimensions of our being. Although I cannot say what life in such a situation would be like, I can nevertheless make some negative statements about it. For example, given that we have by definition the perfect community, any action of a person in that community which did not place the community first as an absolute value would be wrong. This person would have rejected the perfect community, and would therefore be culpable in a sense closer to the sin of Adam and Eve than to our ordinary, everyday imperfect attempts at wickedness. The person's failure in community would have an absoluteness about it. I would suggest that, while Marx is not himself a totalitarian, his assurance about the human achievement of the ideal society leaves the door open to the introduction of absolute ideas about the relation of a person to his community. It is this absoluteness which formulations such as that of Jacques Maritain of the distinction between our being *individuals*, in which sense we are subordinate to the welfare of our human group, and our being *persons*, in which sense we transcend the claims and finality of any given set of human institutions,[226] are attempting to contest. I do not suggest that all who see this problem in Marx's system will necessarily accept the details of Maritain's alternative; what I do suggest is that the realisation that humanity cannot by itself sustain, even if it once achieved, the ideal society, will point to the need for affirming some sense in which the finality of each human person points beyond the imperfect institutions and community which are characteristic of the human condition.

We may for the moment leave the topic of Marx's notion of community, and consider some criticisms of his ideas in regard to history. Many critics would recognise the merits of Marx's insistence on the fact and possibilities of our historicity, and on the need to create a worthwhile world through human activity, but would claim that his account is exaggerated or incomplete. Rotenstreich, for example, says that Marx 'set up history as a total reality and erased the meta-historical reality of man.'[227]

Jean Ladrière argues that 'it is not sufficient to remark that . . . I have a unique and original fashion of living history, that I introduce into it a co-efficient irreducibly "mine". . . . It must be added that the content which I find in my participa-

tion in history is not enough to make me . . . that it is incapable
of fulfilling the expectation of which I am constituted.'[228]

A similar point is made more than once by Girardi. One of
the arguments which he adduces is the realisation that: 'the
tendency of love to prolong its encounter endlessly is irrevocably
smashed against the wall of death in the moment of supreme
solitude.'[229]

The Marxist, and also certain Christians could reject these
charges on the grounds that they involved either a mistaken
essentialist notion of human fulfilment abstracted from concrete
human reality, or a demand for fulfilment over and above the
only one we may reasonably demand and expect—namely,
that of living a life dedicated to the realisation of the kingdom,
or both. But where the Marxist would appear to be on less
firm ground, and where even the Christian Marxist would
have to question Marx's account, is in relation to a question
which I have already referred to: the ability of humanity, by
its own efforts, firstly to attain, and then to maintain, the
perfect community.[230] Perhaps it *is* a kind of essentialist
individualism to want more than to live and die for the
realisation of the perfect community; it is quite different,
however, where we realise that we need some guarantee more
powerful and sure even than human goodwill of the fundamental values which inform and direct our life.

If all we can be sure of is that we can make realistic attempts
at revolution, and real anticipations of the post-revolutionary
situation, then we must accept that the perfection of species-
being can perhaps be advanced, but may well be left tragically
incomplete. If this is the case, then we must concede that the
realisation of genuine efforts to achieve communist society
must be assured if our actions, directed towards and made
meaningful by it, are to be other than isolated sparks in a fire
which just failed to catch.

Marxism and Christianity

I have already in this chapter referred to Christianity as
Marxism's chief competitor in the area of the philosophy of
man, or, to use MacIntyre's phrase, the interpretation of
existence. By this I mean to suggest not so much that
Christianity and Marxism are necessarily and totally opposed:

rather is it the case that each offers a total interpretation of existence, a basic orientation to the world, and that at least on some questions these orientations are contrary.

Marx himself is clearly aware, as we can see especially in Chapter 2, of his radical contesting of the fundamentals of the Christian religion. His philosophy is one of the major stages, noted by Patrick Masterson, in the process whereby religion increasingly came to be considered as a barrier to a more and more optimistic project of secular rationality.[231] Marx's thought is, indeed, the high point of what we may term optimistic, positive atheism. The crucial thing about this kind of atheism is that it discards rather than rejects religion, confident that human fulfilment is indeed possible, but that it can be achieved by humanity alone, and only thus. As Masterson goes on to show, this optimistic project is now less sure of its achievement and of maintaining whatever achievements it may register. It is not my aim, nor would I be competent, to duplicate the analysis of the different types of atheism, and the logic of their sequence, which Masterson presents. I shall take it as a starting-point that events since the turn of the century, and the philosophic reflection of that experience on both the collective and personal planes, issue validly in a dimunition, or even an abandonment, of the optimism characteristic of the nineteenth-century atheist position. My concern is with the reaction of different interpretations of existence to this development.

The logic of the sequence of atheist positions since the seventeenth century, as Masterson interprets it, is that the affirmation of God has increasingly come to be seen as alienating man, as diminishing him. This movement implied, and was in turn reinforced by, the growth in secular optimism. With the development of the existentialist atheist outlook, however, a peculiar irony emerges: here atheism loses its optimistic assurance about the human project, and is in a sense at one with Christianity in pointing to, even if it does not recognise, the need for a transcendent ground beyond the limitations of human efficacy and fidelity.

Can the Marxist recognise this need without abandoning the basis of his outlook and values? It would seem that he cannot. If he realises that the cooling of the earth, the atomic bomb, or human frailty make the secular fulfilment of this possibility far from certain, then there are data of which he cannot make sense. I do not mean in any way to belittle the Marxist optimism, or to suggest that it is naïve. There are, indeed, good grounds for saying that a Christianity or other philosophy of man which does not go *beyond* Marxism, and in a sense develop through the commitment and deficiencies of the Marxist position, has not begun to answer the challenge of our time in the form in which it is authentically presented.

What I do suggest is that, if we are to attempt to answer that challenge, while at the same time realising that we are insufficient alone to meet it fully, then our Marxism, if we are solely and simply Marxists, is valuable but possibly invalid, its project surely worthwhile but not necessarily assured. It is here that we can perhaps quarrel with Marx's treatment of the questions of death and creation. Marx tells us that:

death seems to be a harsh victory of the species over the individual and to contradict their unity; but the particular individual is only a determinate species-being and as such he is mortal. (B 158–9)

The reaction bred by our culture is to say 'This just isn't good enough: we want more out of death than that.' But perhaps even the Christian, if he reflects deeply enough, will grant that this is, in a sense, indeed enough: to live, and if necessary to die, for a reality which is unquestionably worthwhile, emerges as an analytic definition of fulfilment. In other words, certain criticisms of Marx's outlook made by Christians may well err by their essentialism and individualism. The point, however, is not quite so simple if we turn our attention to the question of what guarantee we have of realising our project. Here Masterson formulates the point precisely: that the human moral project, or moral order, while self-justifying, is not necessarily self-validating:[232] we can be certain that it is worth promoting, but not that it will certainly be promoted and sustained. This problem, Masterson claims, can be met only by an affirmation of God.[233] This is the point which, he claims, the existentialist atheist highlights negatively, and the Christian, positively; the Marxist must reject it.

But is he not right to do so? Does not this affirmation take

away from the commitment which we should have to the
creation of a truly human, truly social community? If the
affirmation of God amounts to a concern with one's self which
makes personal development thinkable apart from the creation
of community, if it is orientation to a totally other world,
away from the concerns and needs of our community, then
the Marxist is correct in rejecting it. But there are good grounds
for arguing that what he is rejecting is a deformation of the
Christian position. This latter is not, as it is often taken to be,
a kind of wistful, superior pessimism. It demands as fully as
does Marxism an active commitment to making human history.
At the same time, however, it recognises the inadequacy of
this commitment and this history on their own. It is here that
we can say that Marx, while perhaps correctly rejecting a
version of the idea of creation,[234] misses a point: creation is
more important as a guarantee of where we are going than
as a story of where we came from. Faith in the God of the
doctrine of creation can be an indispensable encouragement,
rather than an insuperable obstacle, to involvement in humanising existence. The difference between the Christian and the
Marxist is not that one does particular kinds of things which
the other does not do, but rather that there is a kind of
realisation of ultimate hopelessness which, logically at least,
should give the Marxist pause, but which is *built into* the
hopeful affirmation of the Christian. The Christian affirmation,
to repeat Masterson's analysis, arises from the realisation that
what is self-justifying, the human moral project, is not self-
validating: it expresses the realisation that if we are going to
go on consistently pursuing this project, we must accept the
only kind of ground which it could have.

To accept this ground is not to make fewer, or even different
kinds of, efforts: it is however to have faced and answered a
question even more fundamental than the Marxist analysis
prompts. It is to state that there are no human circumstances
in which the pursuit of the kingdom would not be the appropriate course of action. This conviction is the manifestation of
the 'complacency' of which Frederick Crowe speaks, when he
says that, 'to a human existence whose structure is simply
defined by care, one opposes not only the hope that modifies
care from within, but a complacency that offsets care from

without and reduces it to a subordinate rank below a prior correspondence with being.'[235]

I do not suggest that Crowe's analysis of complacency and concern is correct in every detail; I have an idea that a Christian Marxist would have much with which to quarrel in it and its presuppositions. But it does make well the point which I have been developing here: concern is the subjective correlative of the self-justifying moral project of humanity, complacency that of the divine assurance that our authentic efforts will not be pointless. Each moment is needed, and Crowe himself recognises that his analysis has to a large extent stated rather than resolved a problem with this notion of complacency, which: 'cannot fail to have an expanding impact whose force and range are hard at the moment to predict, and whose complexity, especially when we consider the interaction of complacency and concern on one another, renders any simple outline impossible.'[236]

Conclusion

I SHALL not in this conclusion summarise the contents of the whole book. I shall simply raise some of the points of interest which have emerged in the course of our study.

The first of these has been stated already at such length that it requires but brief treatment here. It concerns the development of Marx's theory of class warfare. We saw in Chapter 2 that he *develops* from a radical democratic analysis of the dichotomy of state and civil society to a socialist analysis of the antithesis of labour and capital. This analysis should dispel what appears to be a popular impression, of which not all commentators are innocent, that Marx's theory of classes was well-nigh congenital. This point is of more than passing interest. As we have seen, to miss it would blind us to the basic intention, the creation of a community of free social beings, which Marx carries over from his earlier democratic analysis, and which he embodies in the proletariat.

Perhaps the most neglected of all aspects of Marx's early development is the economic aspect. In Chapter 3 we discussed his first economic model, and situated it in the perspective of his development as an economic thinker. Here once more our study should correct an easy but incorrect impression. This is the impression that Marx at some quite late stage in his career suddenly 'became' an economist and stopped being something else. In Chapter 1 we have already noted Marx's rejection of 'theological' polemic, and his interest in a more empirically-based social analysis. This latter translates itself, in the *EPM*, into his first economic studies. Thus Marx's interest in economics is a feature of his earliest positive statements, and not something to which he was 'converted' at some later stage.

One aspect of Marx's early ideas which appears not to have been developed in the later period is the theory of human activity which we elucidated in Chapter 4. We did observe, however, that the tension between labour and truly human activity appears to persist into his later thought. The recurrence of the notion of a post-economic 'realm of true human freedom' in the last volume of *Das Kapital* would suggest that Marx retained at least the basic intention which underlay the earlier theory of human activity.

Perhaps the most crucial question of all for anyone trying to obtain a correct overall perspective on Marx's work is that of determinism and freedom in his notion of history. In the *Essays and EPM* the theory of economic determinism is conspicuous mainly by its absence. And herein lies, paradoxically, the relevance of these writings to that theory. In the *Essays and EPM* we observe the development of Marx's notion of praxis. The problem of determinism in Marx is precisely the problem of reconciling the notions of history and of praxis. Without a correct understanding of the genesis and full implications of this latter notion, we cannot hope either to grasp or to solve the problems connected with the former.

Perhaps the best way to close this account is in referring to an article which belongs properly to the 'Paris period', but which has not received either detailed analysis or lengthy exposition in the preceding chapters. This is the piece 'Critical Remarks on the Article: The King of Prussia and Social Reform', which Marx published in *Vorwärts!* in August 1844. Arnold Ruge is 'the Prussian' who, in a previous issue of that journal, wrote pseudonymously the article which Marx here analyses. Marx's critique is now available in English translation. [237]

We need not go into the details of Marx's and Ruge's interpretation of a cabinet order made by the Prussian king after a workers' revolt in Silesia: what is of interest to us is how the general premises of that rejection show Marx applying to a concrete and specific social question the philosophical and scientific ideas whose development we have just finished studying. He employs the distinction between a social and a merely political revolution, saying that

an industrial revolt can therefore be as partial as it likes, it contains within it a universal soul. . . . A social revolution, even though it be limited to a single industrial district, involves the standpoint of the whole.[238]

He rejects the alleged distinction between 'religious' and 'political' sentiment and motivations, repeating the point, which we have already seen in Chapter 2, about the fundamental similarity between the state and the religious conception of heaven: each is an abstract realm, an escape from the possibility of real, fundamental *social* revolution. He illustrates the blindness of even a well-intentioned bourgeoisie, and of bourgeois political economy, in the face of the condition of the proletariat. This article, in being an application, is also a gathering together, of the main themes of Marx's thought in the Paris period. In this sense it looks not simply back, to the studies of the previous two years, but also forward to the even more profound and detailed empirical study which was to issue in the *Grundrisse* of fifteen years later, and *Das Kapital* of twenty-five years later. It underlines the point with which I shall conclude: that the Paris period is a stage in a process, and must be seen and studied as much from this perspective as for the intrinsic merits of the Paris writings.

Appendix 1

TEXTS AND TRANSLATIONS

THE *Marx-Engels Historisch-Kritische Gesamtausgabe* was published between 1927 and 1932. A full edition of Marx's and Engels' works was planned but, as can be seen from Appendix 2 below, it was not completed. *MEGA* does, however, contain the *Essays and EPM. MEGA* I, 1, i was published at Frankfurt in 1927; I, 3 was published at Berlin in 1932.

Apart from the original publication of the *Essays* in 1844 this was the first publication of the *Essays and EPM.* At the moment there are available four translations into English, only one of which is complete and continuous.

Martin Milligan has published a translation of the *EPM* (Moscow 1959, reprinted 1967). This is based on the *MEGA* text, and the Publisher's Note on page 5 of the volume tells us that 'corrections were made of typographical errors and the author's obvious slips spotted by the Institute of Marxism-Leninism of the Central Committee of the CPSU.' We are not told, however, what were these errors and slips.

In their *Writings of the Young Marx on Philosophy and Society* (New York 1967) Loyd Easton and Kurt Guddat translate the *Essays* in full. They have translated part of the *EPM.* They omit all those parts which we have considered in Chapter 3 under the heading 'Economic Analysis' as does McLellan's translation in *Karl Marx: Early Texts* (Oxford 1971). I would suggest that this is somewhat unwise, as such a presentation of the *EPM* might tend to give an unbalanced impression of Marx as a 'philosopher' pure and simple, and lead us to miss the point that even at this early stage of his career Marx saw economics, philosophy and other disciplines as part of one general inquiry directed toward the 'science of man'. Both the Easton and Guddat and the McLellan versions also omit some of the sections of the *EPM* covered by Chapter 4. The Easton and Guddat version is based on the *MEGA* edition. In their Preface (pp. v–vi) they tell us that where they had doubts about this edition's accuracy they consulted the original manuscripts, and the first edition of the *Essays*, at the International Institute of Social History in Amsterdam. They have also consulted other editions of Marx published in German after the *MEGA*. Their book unfortunately does not contain a discussion of the doubts they encountered or of the corrections which they were led to make in the *MEGA* version, which is to be regretted. (This omission may not occur in the hardcover edition, but the paperback edition refers to the hardcover without indicating any difference of content.)

Professor T. B. Bottomore has translated the *Essays and EPM* (*Karl Marx: Early Writings*, London 1963). He used the 1844 *Deutsch-Französische Jahrbücher* edition of the *Essays*. He has informed me that there is no significant difference between this latter and the *MEGA* version of the *Essays*, a point which is borne out, as far as I have been able to ascertain, with the exception of alternative translation *(d)* cited below. He has used the *MEGA* version of the *EPM*. In the course of preparing this book, I have read the *Essays and EPM* in the *MEGA*, comparing each sentence with its translation in Bottomore. I have relied throughout on Langenscheidt's *Concise German Dictionary* (London 1968). On the basis of this reading, I put forward the following observations and suggestions in relation to Bottomore's translation:

Alternative translations

   (a) The word 'widerspruchslos' occurs at least four times in the *Essays*. The direct translation of this word would be 'contradiction-less' or 'non-contradictory'; where it is used as an adverb, the English version would change accordingly. Marx uses the word on all four occasions as a term in his comparison of political and human emancipation. This, as we have seen, is based on the *contradiction* between state and civil society. The word has been translated in the Bottomore version as follows:

   MEGA I, 1, i, 'Die politische Emanzipation nicht die durchgeführte, die *widerspruchslose* Weise der menschlichen Emanzipation ist.' (582)
   Bottomore: 'Political emancipation is not the final and *absolute* form of human emancipation.' (B 10)

   MEGA (*ibid*) 'als das wirkliche, *widerspruchslose* Gattungsleben des Menschen.' (587)
   Bottomore: 'as the genuine and *harmonoius* species-life of man.' (B 16)

MEGA (ibid) 'ohne euch vollständig und *widerspruchslos* vom Judentum loszusagen.' (591)

Bottomore: 'without renouncing Judaism completely and *absolutely*'. (B 21)

MEGA (ibid): 'die *widerspruchslose* und positive Aufhebung der Religion.' (592)

Bottomore: 'the *consistent* and positive abolition of religion.' (B 23)

The versions offered by this translation are correct, and preferable on grounds of style to a literal translation of this word. I believe, however, that translators should, perhaps in a footnote, refer to the original German word. Human emancipation is 'consistent', 'harmonious' 'full' and so forth, because it abolishes the *contradiction* of state and civil society. Marx's use of the notion of contradiction is both precise and significant. We have seen in Chapter 4 (p. 65 above) that the contradiction within each man's life and conciousness between state and civil society is translated into a contradiction between specific and exclusive socio-economic groups. I suggest that English translations should refer more precisely to the former contradiction.

(b) In *MEGA* I, 1, i, p. 599 there is a quotation in French from Rousseau, in which the phrase 'forces propres' occurs. On the same page, Marx himself uses the French phrase, and is referring explicitly to Rousseau. Bottomore puts 'forces propres' in brackets on the second occasion, but, as he translates the quotation from Rousseau into English, he fails to make this reference clear (B 30, 31). I would suggest that 'forces propres' should either be given in its own right, or put in brackets after 'own powers', on both occasions, so as to clarify this point.

(c) In *MEGA* I, 1, i, p. 614, Marx uses the term 'die Praxis', in the context of the discussion on achieving change in political conditions in Germany. Bottomore translates this as 'practice' (B 52). It would perhaps be worth while to put the original German in brackets after this translation. Easton and Guddat do so. (257)

(d) Since the publication of Professor Bottomore's translation in 1963, a new reading has been established of an important word in the original German of the *EPM*. *MEGA* had transliterated as 'Geist' (i.e., 'mind') an obscure scrawl, which has now been shown to be in fact 'Genuss' (i.e., 'satisfaction'). This revision is referred to, for example, on pages 77, 78, 79, 80, 89 and 92 of *Karl Marx:*

Texte zu Methode und Praxis: II Pariser Manuskripte 1844 (Rowohlt, Hamburg 1968). The corresponding pages in Bottomore are 157 (lines 15 and 16, and lines 27 to 33); 158 (line 33); 160 (line 18); 171 (line 6) and 174 (line 28). On line 6 of page 171 Bottomore does in fact translate the word as 'enjoyment'; elsewhere, however, he follows the *MEGA* version, and gives 'spirit' or 'mind'.

The revision is not without philosophical implications. It involves the difference between an 'idealist' word like 'mind' with its connotations of man's 'abstract, speculative being', and the more down-to-earth, Feuerbachian and 'sensuous' notion of 'satisfaction' or enjoyment. Neither Bottomore's translation and commentary nor this present analysis, however, have argued for a significant 'idealist' influence on Marx, which reveals itself in the passages in question: the revision, therefore, is important as regards translation but does not alter significantly the interpretation and analysis presented here. For this reason, it has not been introduced into or referred to in the body of the text.

(e) On page 44 of his translation, Bottomore gives: 'Religion is only the illusory sun *about which man revolves* so long as he does not revolve about himself.'

Easton and Guddat give: 'Religion is only the illusory sun *that revolves around man* so long as he does not revolve about himself.' (251)

McLellan (116) agrees with this latter version. Having checked the translations with the *MEGA* original, I am satisfied that these latter two translations are correct, and Bottomore mistaken, on this point. I did not draw attention to it in the course of my analysis in Chapter 2, as no point of substance was involved.

Omissions

I have suggested to Professor Bottomore that there are the following omissions in his translation:

(a) In *MEGA* I, 1, i, the last of the Essays ends with: 'Wenn alle inneren Bedingungen erfüllt sind, wird der deutsche Auferstehungsakt verkundet werden durch das Schmettern des gallischen Hahns.' (621)

Easton and Guddat translate this as: 'When all the inner conditions are fulfilled, the day of German resurrection will be announced by the crowing of the French rooster.' (264) The passage should appear at the end of page 59 of Bottomore.

(b) *MEGA* I, 3, p. 92 has this passage: 'Arbeitslohn ist eine unmittelbare Folge der entfremdeten Arbeit, und die entfremdete Arbeit ist die unmittelbare Ursache des Privateigentums. Mit der einen musst daher auch die andere Seite fallen.'

Easton and Guddat render this as: 'Wages are a direct result of alienated labor, and alienated labor is the direct cause of private property. The downfall of one is necessarily the downfall of the other.' (299)

The passage is omitted in Bottomore; it should appear on page 132 of his translation. There is no essential point of Marx's thought contained in this passage which appears nowhere else; as can be seen from Chapter 4, the interconnexions of alienated labour, private property and wages are stated at length in Marx's argument. Thus, while not rendering Bottomore's translation less effective in any essential respect, this omission is an oversight which could be remedied in any later editions.

(c) In *MEGA* I, 3, p. 162, there occurs the sentence: 'Die Geschichte ist die wahre Naturgeschichte des Menschen.'

This sentence, which should occur on page 208 of Bottomore, is omitted from it. Easton and Guddat give: 'History is the true natural history of mankind.' (327)

Again this omission does not mean that we miss any vital point which Marx does not make in the preceding and succeeding arguments. The context is Marx's argument that man can be known only through his history, and his insistence on the oneness (in principle) of man and nature.

(d) *MEGA* I, 3, pp. 162–3 has: 'Diese Nichtigkeit desselben hat für das Bewusstsein nicht nur eine negative, sondern eine positive Bedeutung, denn jene Nichtigkeit des Gegenstands ist eben die selbstbestätigung der Ungegenständlichkeit, der Abstraktion seiner Selbst.'

This passage is omitted from p. 209 of Bottomore.

Easton and Guddat give: 'This nullity of the object has not merely a negative but also a positive meaning for consciousness because it is precisely the self-confirmation of non-objectivity, of the abstraction of itself.' (327)

As the reader will see from Chapter 5, this sentence adds nothing essentially new to Marx's argument that Hegel misconceives the world, man and the relation of man to the world. Nevertheless, as its omission appears to be due to simple oversight rather than to any textual or other similar consideration, it should be rectified in any future editions of the translation.

Manuscript Number Four

An appendix to *MEGA* I, 3 (pp. 592–6) contains a short manuscript written by Marx in Paris in 1844. The editors of *MEGA* have given it the title: 'Marx's excerpts from the last chapter of Hegel's *Phenomenology of Mind*'.

Bottomore (p. xviii), Easton and Guddat (p. 283) and McLellan (p. 130) refer to this manuscript. They do not translate it. I have made a rough translation of this manuscript for my own purposes, but believe that these translators are justified in their omission. What is involved is a re-production of the greater part of the final chapter of Hegel's *Phenomenology of Mind*. Marx sometimes abbreviates Hegel, and sometimes makes interjections in the tone of the argument which we have reviewed in Chapter 5. There is no point in the manuscript which does not emerge in the criticism of Hegel which we have already seen, and for which Manuscript Number 4 is a preparatory exercise.

Appendix 2

A BIBLIOGRAPHY OF MAJOR WORKS OF BAUER, FEUERBACH, HEGEL AND MARX

N.B. In the case of Bauer, Feuerbach and Hegel, we give titles of English translations of their works in brackets. Each title appearing in brackets *directly* after a German title is that of an English translation of that German work.

Bruno Bauer (1808–82):
Kritik der evangelischen Geschichte der Synoptiker, 3 vols, Leipzig 1841–42.
Die Posaune des jungsten gerichts über Hegel den Atheisten und Antichristen, Leipzig 1841.
Die Judenfrage, Braunschweig 1843.
Das Entdecke Christentum, Zurich and Winterthur 1843.

Ludwig Feuerbach (1804–72):
Sämtliche Werke, ed. W. Bolin and F. Jodl, Stuttgart 1959.
Das Wesen des Christentums, 2nd ed. Leipzig 1834 (translated as *Essence of Christianity* by Marian Evans, London 1853, Paperback edition New York 1957).
'Vorläufige Thesen zur Reformation der Philosophie' in *Anekdota zur neuesten deutschen Philosophie*, ed. Arnold Ruge, 1843.
Grundsätze der Philosophie der Zukunft, 1843.

Georg Hegel (1770–1831);
Die Phänomonologie des Geistes, 1807 (*The Phenomenology of Mind*, E. tr. J. B. Baillie, London and New York 1966).
(*The Logic of Hegel, translated from the Encyclopaedia of the Philosophical Sciences*, E. tr. W. Wallace, Oxford 1892. This includes sections on Nature)
(*The Philosophy of History*, E. tr. J. Sibree, New York 1899)
Grundlinien der Philosophie des Rechts, 1821 (*The Philosophy of Right*, translated and annotated by T. M. Knox, Oxford 1942).

KARL HEINRICH MARX (1818–1881)

1841

Doctoral Dissertation, *Differenz der demokritischen und epikurischen Naturphilosophie*
MEGA Abteilung 1, Band 1.
Translated in part in N. Livergood, *Activity in Marx's Philosophy*, The Hague 1967

1842–43

Articles in *Rheinische Zeitung*
MEGA 1, 1.
Some translated in Easton and Guddat (editors and translators), *Writings of the Young Marx on Philosophy and Society*, New York 1967, and in D. McLellan, *Karl Marx: Early Texts*, Oxford 1971

Kritik des Hegelschen Staatrecht
MEGA 1, 1.
Translated in part in Easton and Guddat, *op. cit.* and in McLellan, *op. cit.*

1843([239])

Articles in *Anekdota zur neuesten deutschen Philosophie* (ed. Arnold Ruge)
MEGA 1. 1.
Translated in Easton and Guddat, *op. cit.* and in McLellan, *op. cit.*

1844([240])

Correspondence with Bakunin, Feuerbach and Ruge, and essays, in *Deutsch-Französische Jahrbücher*
MEGA 1, 1.
Correspondence translated in part and essays translated in full, in Easton and Guddat, *op. cit.* and in McLellan *op. cit.* Essays translated in T. B. Bottomore, (ed. and tr.), *Karl Marx: Early Writings*, London 1963

Economic and Philosophical Manuscripts
MEGA 1, 3.
Translated in Bottomore, *op. cit.*, and also in M. Milligan, *Economic and Philosophical Manuscripts*, Moscow 1959
Translated in part in Easton and Guddat, *op. cit.* and in McLellan, *op. cit.*

Articles in *Vorwärts!*
MEGA 1, 3.
One article translated in Easton and Guddat, *op. cit.* and in
McLellan, *op. cit.*

1845
Die Heilige Familie (with Engels)
MEGA 1, 3.
The Holy Family, E. tr. Dixon, Moscow 1956

Theses on Feuerbach
MEGA 1, 3.
First published (in German) by Engels in 1888. Translated into
English in:
Karl Marx: Selected Writings, ed. Bottomore and Rubel, London
1965
The Marxists by C. Wright Mills, London 1963
Basic Problems of Marx's Philosophy by Nathan Rotenstreich,
Indianapolis 1965
The German Ideology (translated by various persons; see p. 5 of
the volume), Moscow 1968

1846
Die Deutsche Ideologie (with Engels)
MEGA 1, 5.
The German Ideology (translated by various persons; see p. 5 of the
volume) Moscow 1968

1847
Misère de la Philosophie
MEGA 1, 6.
The Poverty of Philosophy (translator's name not given) Moscow
1956

1848
Manifest der Kommunistischen Partei (with Engels)
MEGA 1, 6.
Communist Manifesto: Socialist Landmark E. tr. 1930 E. and C.
Paul. With Introduction by H. J. Laski, London 1948
The Communist Manifesto, Reproduction of the translation made
in 1888 by Samuel Moore, under the supervision of Engels.
With Introduction by A. J. P. Taylor. London 1967

1857–58
Grundrisse der Kritik der politischen Ökonomie (Rodentwurf)
  MEGA does not include this work.
  Published Moscow 1939, Berlin 1953.
  One section translated as *Pre-Capitalist Economic Formations*,
  edited with introduction by E. J. Hobsbawm (1964)
  Selections translated with introduction, in D. McLellan, (ed.
  and tr.) *Marx's Grundrisse*, London 1971

1859
Zur Kritik der Politischen Ökonomie
  MEGA does not include this work.
  First German edition Berlin 1859. German edition edited by
  K. Kautsky, including 'Introduction' omitted from 1859 edition,
  Stuttgart 1907
  A Contribution to the Critique of Political Economy, translated by
  N. I. Stone from Kautsky's edition, 1909
  'Introduction' published in English in Horowitz (ed.) *Marx and
  Modern Economics* London, 1968

1867 onwards
Das Kapital
  MEGA does not include this work.
  For bibliographical details of German editions and English
  translations of this work, we refer the reader to Bottomore and
  Rubel (eds.) *Karl Marx: Selected Writings*, Pelican London 1965
  pp. 267–8

Appendix 3

Select Bibliography

Adams, H. P., *Karl Marx in his Earlier Writings,* New York 1965.

Althusser, L., 'Contradiction and Overdetermination' in *New Left Review* 41 (1967) 15–35;
„   *Pour Marx,* Paris 1965.

Avineri, S., *The Social and Political Thought of Karl Marx,* C. U. P. 1968.

Barker, E., *Principles of Social and Political Theory,* Oxford 1956.

Barrett, W., *Irrational Man,* New York 1962.

Berlin, I., *Karl Marx,* London 1965.

Bigo, P., *Marxisme et Humanisme,* Paris 1961.

Calvez, J. Y., *La Pensée de Karl Marx,* Paris 1956.

Carr, E. H., *What is History?* London 1967.

Collins, J. D., *The Existentialists,* Chicago 1952.

Cooper, R., *The Logical Influence of Hegel on Marx,* Seattle 1925.

Copleston, F. C., *History of Philosophy,* Vol. 7 Part II, New York 1965.

Cottier, G., *L'Athéisme du jeune Marx,* Paris 1959.

Crowe, F., 'Complacency and Concern in the Thought of St. Thomas' in *Theological Studies,* Vol. 20 Nos. 1 (March 1959) 1–39; 2 (June 1959) 198–290; and 3 (September 1959) 343–81.

Delfgaauw, B., *The Young Marx,* London 1967.

Dobb, M., *Marx as an Economist,* London 1943.

Doyon, J., *Le concept d'aliénation religieuse dans Marx,* Sherbrooke 1966.

Dupré, L., *Philosophical Foundations of Marxism,* New York 1966.

Emmett, W. H., *The Marxian Economic Handbook and Glossary,* 1925.

Engels, F., *Selected Writings,* London 1967.

Findlay, J. N., *Hegel: A Re-examination,* London 1964.

Friedmann, G., *The Anatomy of Work,* London 1961.

Friedrich, M., *Philosophie und Ökonomie beim jungen Marx,* Berlin 1960.

Fromm, E., *Marx's Concept of Man*, New York 1969;
„   *Escape from Freedom*, New York 1941.

Garaudy, R., *Humanisme Marxiste*, Paris 1957.
Gauthier, R. A., *Magnanimité: l'ideal de la grandeur dans la philosophie païenne et dans la théologie chrétienne*, Paris 1951.
Gilby, T., *Between Community and Society*, London 1955.
Ginsberg, M., *The Psychology of Society*, London 1924.
Girardi, G., *Marxism and Christianity*, Dublin 1968.
Grégoire, F., *Aux sources de la pensée de Marx: Hegel, Feuerbach*, Louvain 1947.

Heaton, H., *Economic History of Europe*, New York 1948.
Heimann, E., *History of Economic Doctrines*, New York 1964.
Horowitz, D. (ed.), *Marx and Modern Economics*, London 1968.
Kamenka, E., *Ethical Foundations of Marxism*, London 1962.
Kangrga, M., 'Das Problem der Entfremdung in Marx' Werk' in *Praxis* 3ème année, No. 4, Zagreb 1967, 13–30.
Koestler, A., (et al.), *The God that Failed*, London 1950.
Kolakowski, L., *Marxism and Beyond*, London 1968.
Koren, H. J., *Marx and the Authentic Man*, Duquesne 1967.
Kuczynski, J., *The Rise of the Working Class*, London 1967.
Kwant, R., *The Philosophy of Labour*, Louvain 1960.

Ladrière, J., 'History and Destiny' in *Philosophy Today*, X.
Lefebvre, H., *Marx, sa vie, son oeuvre avec un exposé de sa philosophie*, Paris 1964.
Livergood, N., *Activity in Marx's Philosophy*, The Hague 1967.
Lonergan, B., *Insight*, New York 1968.
Löwith, K., *From Hegal to Nietzsche*, New York 1964;
„   'Man's Self-alienation in the Early Writings of Marx' in *Social Research* XXI (1954) 204–31.
Luijpen, H., *Phenomenology and Atheism*, Louvain 1964.
Lukàcs, G., *Existentialisme ou Marxisme?* Paris 1948;
„   'Zur philosophischen Entwicklung des jungen Marx' in *Deutsche Zeitschrift für Philosophie*, Vol. 2 No. 2 (1954) 288–343.

McLellan, D., *The Young Hegelians and Karl Marx*, London 1969;
„   *Marx before Marxism*, London 1970.
MacMurray, J., *The Self as Agent*, New York 1957.
Marcuse, H., *Negations*, London 1968;
„   *Reason and Revolution*, London 1968.

Maritain, J., *The Person and the Common Good*, Notre Dame, 1966.
Masterson, P., *Atheism and Alienation*, Dublin 1971.
Mende, G., *Karl Marx' Entwicklung vom revolutionären Demokraten zum Kommunisten*, Berlin 1960.
Meyer, A., *Marxism the Unity of Theory and Practice*, Oxford 1954.
Murry, J. M. (et al.), *Marxism*, London 1935.
Mills, C.W., *The Marxists*, London 1963.

Nicolaus, M., 'The Unknown Marx' in *New Left Review* 48 (1968) 41–61.
Novak, M., *Belief and Unbelief: A Philosophy of Self-knowledge*, London 1966.

Pappenheim, F., *The Alienation of Modern Man*, New York 1959.
Popitz, H., *Der entfremdete Mensch*, Basle 1953.

Reardon, M., *Religious Thought in the Nineteenth Century*, C. U. P. 1966.
Robinson, E. A. G., *The Structure of Competitive Industry*, C. U. P. 1959.
Robinson, J., *On Re-reading Marx*, London 1953.
   „   *Economic Philosophy*, London 1962;
   „   *An Essay on Marxian Economics*, New York 1966.
Rotenstreich, N., *Basic Problems of Marx's Philosophy*, Indianapolis/ New York 1965.
Russell, B. (et al.), *The Meaning of Marxism*, New York 1934.

Schumpeter, J., *History of Economic Analysis*, New York 1954.
Simpson, M., 'The "Death of God" Theology: Some Philosophical Reflections' in *Heythrop Journal*, October 1969, 371–89.
Somerhausen, L., *L'humanisme agissant de Karl Marx*, Paris 1946.
Stace, W. T., *The Philosophy of Hegel*, New York 1955.
Supek, R., 'Karl Marx et l'Époque de l'Automation' in *Praxis* 3ème année No. 4, Zagreb 1967, 31–8.

Thier, E., *Das Menschenbild des jungen Marx*, Göttingen 1961.
Tillich, P., 'Marx's View of History' in S. Diamond (ed.) *Culture in History*, London 1961.
Tucker, R., *Philosophy and Myth in Karl Marx*, Cambridge 1961.
Turner, D., *On the Philosophy of Karl Marx*, Dublin 1968.

Notes

PREFACE

1. Reference will also be made to two additional writings of the Paris period. These are the manuscript notes 'On James Mill', which Marx culled from his economic readings in the Paris period and the article 'Critical Remarks on the Article: The King of Prussia and Social Reform' which he published in the review *Vörwarts!* in Paris in August 1844. These will be discussed chiefly in, respectively, Chapter 4 and the Conclusion. I shall use the rubric of the 'Paris Writings', and other substitutes for it, to refer to the *Essays and EPM* exclusive of the two writings just cited, but do not intend thereby to suggest that they do not fall strictly within the scope of the Paris period.

2. H. Lefebvre, *Marx: sa vie, son oeuvre, avec un exposé de sa philosophie*, P.V.F. 1964, 44.

3. See *Pour Marx*, Paris 1965, throughout.

4. Published in New York 1969.

5. *Ibid.*, 2.

6. 'The Unknown Marx', in *New Left Review* 48 (London 1968) 41–61; see especially p. 60.

7. *Marx's 'Grundrisse'*, London 1971, 12.

8. *Marx before Marxism*, London 1970, 220.

9. M. Milligan, (ed. and tr.) *Economic and Philosophical Manuscripts*, Moscow 1959, reprinted 1967; L. Easton and K. Guddat, (ed. and tr.) *Writings of the Young Marx on Philosophy and Society*, New York 1967; D. McLellan, (ed. and tr.) *Karl Marx: Early Texts*, Oxford 1971.

CHAPTER ONE

10. Throughout this introductory chapter I draw on the following works: D. McLellan, *The Young Hegelians and Karl Marx*, London 1969; *id.*, *Marx before Marxism*, London 1970; I. Berlin, *Karl Marx*, London 1965, especially the earlier chapters; H. P. Adams, *Karl Marx in his Earlier Writings*, New York 1965; G. Lukàcs, 'Zur philosophischen Entwicklung des jungen Marx' in *Deutsche Zeitschrift fur Philosophie* 11/2 (1954), 288–343. I do not refer to these

works specifically except where I have taken direct quotations from them.

11. Ludwig Feuerbach to his father, quoted in McLellan, *Young Hegelians*, 4–5.

12. McLellan, *Young Hegelians*, 1.

13. *The Ethical Foundations of Marxism*, London 1962, 52.

14. McLellan, *Young Hegelians*, 21.

15. McLellan, *Young Hegelians*, 31.

16. *MEGA*, Section I, Volume 1, first half-volume, Frankfurt 1927, 179–393. Some of these articles are translated in Loyd Easton and Kurt Guddat (eds. and trs.) *Writings of the Young Marx on Philosophy and Society*, New York 1967 (paperback edition) 96–142.

17. *MEGA*, I, 1, i, 179–230.

18. *MEGA*, I, 1, i, 212. (Not translated in Easton and Guddat, *op. cit.*)

19. *MEGA*, I, 1, i, 260–66. (Translated in Easton and Guddat, *op. cit.*, 131–5.)

20. *MEGA*, I, 1, i, 266–304. (Not in Easton and Guddat. *op. cit.*)

21. *MEGA*, I, 1, i, 403–553. (In part in Easton and Guddat, *op. cit.*, 151–202.)

22. *MEGA*, I, 1, i, 406; quotation is from Easton and Guddat, *op. cit.*, 155.

23. *MEGA*, I, 1, i, 410.

24. *MEGA*, I, 1, i, 412: 'Das einzige Interesse ist "die Idee" schlechthin, die "logische Idee" . . . wiederzufinden.' Easton and Guddat give (*op. cit.*, 161): 'The main thing is to rediscover "the Idea" itself, the "logical Idea".'

25. *MEGA*, I, 1, i, 414. (See Easton and Guddat, *op. cit.*, 163.)

26. *MEGA*, I, 1, i, 476. (Not translated in Easton and Guddat, *op. cit.*)

27. *MEGA*, I, 1, i, 557–75. (Some extracts from this correspondence translated in Easton and Guddat, *op. cit.*, 203–15.)

28. *Karl Marx*, 81.

29. *Philosophical Foundations of Marxism*, New York 1966, 121.

30. See, for example, the article on the young Marx in *Pour Marx*, Paris 1966, 45–83; translated in *For Marx* (E. tr. Brewster, London 1966) pp. 87–128.

31. *The Social and Political Thought of Karl Marx*, London 1968.

32. *La Pensée de Karl Marx*, Paris 1956.

33. *Karl Marx in his Earlier Writings*, New York, 1965 edition.

34. *The Young Marx*, London 1967.

35. *Philosophical Foundations of Marxism*, New York 1966.

36. *Philosophie und Ökonomie beim jungen Marx*, Berlin 1960.

37. *Marxisme et Humanisme*, Paris 1961.

38. *L'Athéisme du jeune Marx*, Paris 1959.

39. *Le Concept d'Aliénation Religieuse dans Marx*, Sherbrooke 1966.

40. *Activity in Marx's Philosophy*, The Hague 1967.

41. *Basic Problems of Marx's Philosophy*, Indianapolis 1965.

42. *On the Philosophy of Karl Marx*, Dublin 1969, 22, 23.

43. See p. 5 above.

CHAPTER TWO

44. Published by Braunschweig, 1843.

45. For further information, see H. M. Sachar, *The Course of Modern Jewish History*, London 1958, especially chapters III, V, VI, and XI.

46. *The Young Hegelians and Karl Marx*, 77.

47. G. Lukàcs, 'Zur philosophischen Entwicklung des jungen Marx' in *Deutsche Zeitschrift für Philosophie* 11/2 (1954), 300.

48. Lukàcs, *Zur . . . Entwicklung*, 300.

49. W. T. Stace, *The Philosophy of Hegel*, Toronto 1955, 105–6.

50. (The capacity of the present-day Jews and Christians to become free), Zurich and Winterthur 1843.

51. *Marx's Concept of Man*, New York 1969, x.

52. *Marx before Marxism*, 142.

53. *The Ethical Foundations of Marxism*, 61, note.

54. Bottomore, xix.

55. *Karl Marx in his Earlier Writings*, 67.

56. *The Social and Political Thought of Karl Marx*, 25.

57. *Ibid.*, 57.

58. *Zur . . . Entwicklung*, 298.

59. *Zur . . . Entwicklung*, 318.

60. Bottomore, xiii.

61. *Zur . . . Entwicklung*, 323.

CHAPTER THREE

62. Bottomore, 69–119; *MEGA*, I, 3, 33–80.

63. On this point, see Bigo, *Marxisme et Humanisme, passim*.

64. *The Marxists*, London 1963, 38.

65. For an evaluation of *Das Kapital* as a model, see M. Bronfenbrenner, 'Das Kapital for the Modern Man' in D. Horowitz (ed.), *Marx and Modern Economics*, London 1968.

66. See E. Heimann, *History of Economic Doctrines*, New York 1964, especially Chapters III and IV.

67. These arguments appear in Bottomore, 69–74.

68. Respectively, *Théorie nouvelle d'économie sociale et politique*, Paris 1842; and *Die Bewegung der Produktion*, Zurich and Winterthur 1843.

69. See E. A. G. Robinson, *The Structure of Competitive Industry*, London 1959, 26, 37, 56, 60, 64.

70. See Heaton, *Economic History of Europe*, New York 1948, chapter XXVI.

71. See Bottomore, 48–9.

72. This is a quotation by Marx from Pecqueur, *op. cit.*

73. 'The Unknown Marx' in *New Left Review* 48 (1968), 41–61. Further light has also been shed by the text and commentary of McLellan's *Marx's Grundrisse*, London 1971, which appeared after this book had been drafted.

74. (Fundamental Traits of a Critique of Political Economy, rough draft), 1857–8.

75. Nicolaus, *Unknown Marx*, 60.

76. *Ibid.*, 60.

77. *Ibid.*, 46.

78. *Ibid.*, 47.

79. *Ibid.*, 51–3.

80. Bottomore, 88.

81. See Horowitz (ed.), *op cit.*, 50.

82. See Bigo, *op. cit.*, 32. This point holds generally of English language rather than continental commentators.

83. (Outlines of a Critique of Political Economy) published 1844 in *Deutsch-französische Jahrbücher*. I use the translation from Engels, *Selected Writings*, London 1967, 148–77.

84. Engels, *Outlines of a Critique*, 154.

85. *Ibid.*, 157.

86. *Ibid.*, 163.

87. *Ibid.*, 168.

88. *Ibid.*, 165–6.

89. *Ibid.*, 172.

90. *Ibid.*, 164, 173, 175.

91. 'On James Mill' in D. McLellan, *Karl Marx: Early Texts*, London 1971, 194.

92. *The Young Marx*, 35.

93. *Philosophical Foundations of Marxism*, 120 (my italics).

94. *Reason and Revolution*, London 1968, 281.

CHAPTER FOUR

95. Marcuse, *Reason and Revolution*, 304.

96. *History of Economic Analysis*, New York 1954, 598.

97. *Marxisme et Humanisme*, 140.

98. *The Ethical Foundations of Marxism*, 70.

99. See Chapter 2, p. 26 above.

100. For a fuller statement of this point, see Chapter 2, pp. 36–8 above.

101. See 'Man's Self-alienation in the Early Writings of Marx' in *Social Research XXI* (1954), 204–31. The quotation is from p. 218.

102. See Chapter 3, p. 52 above.

103. 'On James Mill' in D. McLellan, *Karl Marx: Early Texts*, 197.

104. See Chapter 3, p. 55–8 above.

105. 'On James Mill' in D. McLellan, *Karl Marx: Early Texts*, 196.

106. 'On James Mill' in D. McLellan, *Karl Marx: Early Texts*, 197.

107. Jean-Baptiste Say, *Traité d'économie politique*, Paris 1817.

108. 'On James Mill' in D. McLellan, *Karl Marx: Early Texts*, 198.

109. *Ibid.*, 190.

110. *Ibid.*, 192.

111. See Chapter 2 above, *passim*.

112. 'On James Mill' in D. McLellan, *Karl Marx: Early Texts*, 198–9.

113. *Ibid.*, 202.

114. *Humanisme Marxiste*, Paris 1957, 22.

115. *Ibid.*, 36, note 1.

116. This is a quotation from *Das Kapital* which Friedmann gives on p. 93 of his work, without a reference to its source.

117. *The Anatomy of Work*, London-Melbourne-Toronto 1961, 94.

118. *Ibid.*, 153.

119. This is a quotation from *Das Kapital*, III, given in Bottomore and Rubel (eds.) *Karl Marx: Selected Writings*, London 1965, 260.

120. Marx quotes from Schulz's *Die Bewegung der Produktion*, Zurich and Winterthur 1843, 67–8.

121. *Op. cit.*, 294–5 (my italics).

122. *Op. cit.*, 273–312.

123. See Bigo, *op. cit.*, especially pp. xxxv–xliii.

124. See Chapter XIII of his *Philosophy and Myth in Karl Marx*, London 1961.

125. For a description of the thought of this and other relevant economic schools, see Heimann, *History of Economic Doctrines*.

126. *The Social and Political Thought of Karl Marx*, 118.

127. *Karl Marx in his Earlier Writings*, 109.

128. Kangrga, 'Das Problem der Entfremdung in Marx' Werk', *Praxis* 3ème Année No. 4 (Zagreb 1967), 13–30. The quotation is from p. 18.

CHAPTER FIVE

129. *MEGA*, I, 3, 150–72; Bottomore, 195–219.

130. *Karl Marx' Entwicklung vom revolutionaren Demokraten zum Kommunisten*, Berlin 1960, 141.

131. *The Social and Political Thought of Karl Marx*, 102.

132. See Chapter 2, p. 33 above.

133. 'Theses on Feuerbach' in *The German Ideology*, Moscow 1968.

134. See p. 6 above.

135. See Appendix 2.

136. See Appendix 2.

137. See Appendix 2.

138. See Appendix 2.

139. Findlay, *Hegel: A Re-examination*, London 1964, 348.

140. *Ibid.*, 23–4, 346–54 and *passim*.

141. See Appendix 2.

142. Lukàcs, 'Zur Philosophischen Entwicklung des jungen Marx' in *Deutsche Zeitschrift für Philosophie* 11/2 (1954), 288–343, *passim*.

143. *Der entfremdete Mensch*, Basle 1953, 126.

144. *Philosophie und Ökonomie beim jungen Marx*, Berlin 1960, 137.

CHAPTER SIX

145. See p. 89 above.

146. See p. 32–3 above.

147. See pp. 58–61 above.

148. Bottomore and Rubel (eds.) *Karl Marx: Selected Writings*, 36.

149. See Livergood, *Activity in Marx's Philosophy*, The Hague 1967, especially chapter II.

150. See Chapter 5, p. 92 above.

151. Although as we saw on p. 92 above he does hint at his rejection of crude materialism even in the *EPM*.

152. *Theses on Feuerbach*, translated in Bottomore and Rubel, *op. cit.*, 82–4.

153. *Ibid.*

154. Rotenstreich, *Basic Problems of Marx's Philosophy*, 33.

155. 'Marxism and the Classical Definition of Truth' in Kolakowski, *Marxism and Beyond*, London 1968, 58–86.

156. *Op. cit.*, 85.

157. See Kwant, *De Wijsbegeerte van Karl Marx*, Utrecht 1961, 60–61; quoted in Delfgaauw, *The Young Marx*, 84–5.

158. See Calvez, *La Pensée de Karl Marx*, *passim*; also Copleston, *History of Philosophy*, Vol. 7 Part II, 82–5.

159. See Bottomore, 49–50.

160. See Chapter 5, p. 92 above.

161. *The German Ideology*, Moscow 1968, 51.

162. See 'Marx's View of History' in S. Diamond (ed.), *Culture in History*, London 1961.

163. *Op. cit.*, 135.

164. McLellan, *The Young Hegelians and Karl Marx*, 10.

165. Lukàcs, 'Zur Philosophischen Entwicklung das jungen Marx' in *Deutsche Zeitschrift fur Philosophie*, 11/2 (1954), 288–343.

166. See Chapter 5, p. 86 above.

167. Lukàcs, *Zur . . . Entwicklung*, 326.

168. See Bottomore and Rubel, *op. cit.*, 82.

169. B. Delfgaauw, *The Young Marx*, 50.

170. *Op. cit.*, 102.

171. *The Poverty of Philosophy*, London 1956, 115.

172. *Ibid.*, 122.

173. *Ibid.*, 109.

174. *The German Ideology*, Moscow 1968, 38.

175. *History of Philosophy*, Vol. 7 Part II, 94.

176. *Marx's Concept of Man*, 9.

177. See Bottomore and Rubel, *op. cit.*, 82.

178. Fromm, *op. cit.*, 22.

179. *Ethical Foundations of Marxism*, 142.

180. *Op. cit.*, 138.

181. *Marxism, the Unity of Theory and Practice*, Harvard 1964, 29.

182. *Ibid.*, 24.

183. *Ibid.*, 30.

184. *Ibid.*, Chapter 1 *passim*.

185. *Ibid.*, 42.

186. 'Contradiction and Overdetermination' in *New Left Review* 41 (1967), 15–35. (This article is a translation of one chapter from Althusser's *Pour Marx*, Paris 1965.)

187. *Ibid.*, 25.

188. *Poverty of Philosophy*, 109.

189. *Humanisme Marxiste*, 59.

190. *Poverty of Philosophy*, 110–11.

191. *Contradiction*, 31.

192. *Ibid.*, 32.

193. *Marxisme et Humanisme*, 27.

194. *Reason and Revolution*, London 1968, 273–4.

195. 'Karl Marx et l'Epoque de l'Automation' in *Praxis* 1967 No. 1 (Zagreb), 33.

196. See Chapter 3, pp. 53–5 above. For further discussion of Marx's conception of technology and the change which it permits in the utilisation of time, see the Introduction and commentary in McLellan (ed. and tr.) *Marx's Grundisse*.

197. See Chapter 4, p. 81 above.

198. Quoted in Bottomore and Rubel, *op. cit.*, 260.

199. A quotation from *The German Ideology*, in Bottomore and Rubel, *op. cit.*, 75.

CHAPTER SEVEN

200. See Appendix 1.

201. This work was translated into English by Marian Evans (George Eliot) in 1853, and published as *The Essence of Christianity*, New York 1957.

202. *Idem.*, 23.

203. *Idem.*, 29–30.

204. *Idem.*, 21.

205. For further discussion see McLellan, *The Young Hegelians and Karl Marx*, 1–40, 85–113 and *passim*; see also Luijpen, *Phenomenology and Atheism*, Louvain 1964, Chapter 3; Gregoire, *Aux Sources de la Pensée de Marx: Hegel, Feuerbach*, Louvain 1947, *passim*; and Masterson, *Atheism and Alienation*, Dublin 1971, Chapter 4.

206. Koren, *Marx and the Authentic Man*, Duquesne 1967.

207. See Chapter 3, p. 56 above.

208. *Marx: Economic and Philosophical Manuscripts of 1844* (E. tr. Milligan), Moscow 1967, 106 (footnote).

209. *Philosophy and Myth in Karl Marx*, London 1961, 161 and Chapter 10 throughout.

210. See R. D. Laing, *The Divided Self*, London 1965; and P. Winch, *The Idea of a Social Science*, London 1958.

211. *Marxism and Christianity*, London 1969, 10.

212. *Marxism and Christianity*, 47–8.

213. See p. 126 above.

214. See B 155, and p. 127 above.

215. See p. 103 above.

216. P. Berger, *Invitation to Sociology*, London 1966, 171.

217. Marx and Engels, *German Ideology*, Moscow 1968, 46.

218. See, for example, G. Marcel, *The Mystery of Being*, Chicago 1966; E. Mounier, *Be Not Afraid: Studies in Personalist Sociology*, London 1951.

219. See A. Kenny, *Action, Emotions and Will*, London 1963; P. Winch, *The Idea of a Social Science*, London 1958.

220. See, for example, B. Lonergan, *Insight*, New York 1968, especially chapters 6 and 7; and M. Novak, *Belief and Unbelief*, London 1966.

221. *The Self as Agent*, New York 1957, 29.

222. *The Problem of Method*, London 1963, throughout.

223. See *Invitation to Sociology*, London 1966; and *The Social Construction of Reality* [with Thomas Luckmann], New York 1967.

224. 'Theses on Feurerbach', in *German Ideology*, Moscow 1968, 659.

225. See B 165–7 and B 157–9, and pp. 158–9 above.

226. See *The Person and the Common Good*, Notre Dame 1966.

227. *Basic Problems of Marx's Philosophy*, New York 1965.

228. 'History and Destiny' in *Philosophy Today*, X, 3–25. The quotation is from p. 23.

229. *Marxism and Christianity*, Dublin 1968, 115.

230. In this discussion I have drawn heavily and gratefully on some ideas suggested to me by Herbert McCabe O.P., although he is not responsible for my interpretation or use of these ideas.

231. *Atheism and Alienation*, Dublin 1971, throughout.

232. See the final chapter 'Chiaroscuro of Hope' of the work already cited.

233. *Ibid.*

234. See B 165–7.

235. 'Complacency and Concern in the Thought of St Thomas', in *Theological Studies*, Vol. 20 (1959), 1–39, 198–230 and 343–381. This quotation is from pp. 371–2.

236. *Ibid.*, 355–6.

CONCLUSION

237. D. McLellan (ed. and tr.) *Karl Marx: Early Texts*, 204–21.

238. *Ibid.*, 220.

APPENDIX TWO

239. There is a discrepancy between the dates given by this bibliography and by Easton and Guddat, *op. cit.*, for both the *Deutsch-Französische Jahrbücher* and the *Anekdota* articles; Easton and Guddat give the year of writing, which in each case is the year preceding that of publication, which is given here.

240. See note 1 above.

Index